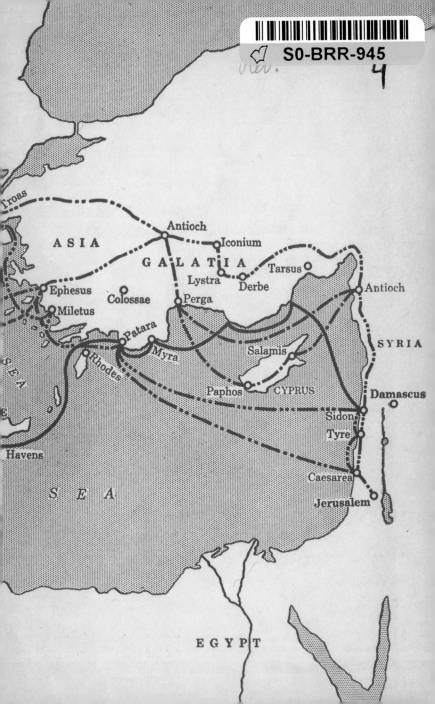

PAUL

FOR EVERYONE

BOOKS BY CHESTER WARREN QUIMBY

Paul for Everyone

The Gospel Today

Jesus As They Remembered Him

The Sermon on the Mount—A Questionnaire

PAUL
FOR EVERYONE

By

CHESTER WARREN QUIMBY

New York

THE MACMILLAN COMPANY

1944

To
ROLLIN
"Beloved and longed for, my joy and crown"
and
MARGARET
"A comfort unto me"

ACKNOWLEDGMENTS

MY GRATITUDE goes to:

Prof. John Knox of Union Theological Seminary for robbing himself of precious vacation hours to read and criticize the manuscript. Also, though plainly pressed for time, for giving himself lavishly as though free in a vast leisure, in a most gracious personal interview.

Prof. Harris Franklin Rall of Garrett Biblical Institute, who literally stole time from more urgent affairs to read the manuscript and make many valuable suggestions.

Dr. Roy L. Smith, Editor of *The Christian Advocate*, for his generous request that he might write The Foreword.

The International Council of Religious Education, owner of the copyright, for permission to quote the Scripture passages from the American Standard Edition of the Revised Bible.

My beloved wife for her unfailing encouragement, innumerable corrections in style, typing the manuscript, and reading the proofs, and, most difficult of all, checking and double-checking the endless Scripture quotations.

FOREWORD

THERE ARE those who declare that modern Christianity is more the product of the mind of Paul than of the life of Christ. It has been charged that the tentmaker of Tarsus has so distorted the simple message of the Galilean Carpenter that there is little resemblance between the two. While this states the case extremely, it must be confessed that the faith which spread across the earth that amazing first century was very different from the teachings of the Galilean, because the first-century preachers had one great basic fact, which Jesus could only anticipate, *The Resurrection!*

This fact began a different Gospel from the one Jesus preached. Whereas Jesus made occasional references to his impending death, he said almost nothing about his resurrection, for throughout his ministry it was still in prospect. But the first-century Church built its faith upon it as an accomplished fact. Here was the rock-base of the new religion, which had to be explained to the Greek mind and the Roman world. Paul himself said, "If Christ hath not been raised, then is our preaching vain." He staked everything on that one simple and staggering fact.

The explanation of this triumph over the tomb, under the Providence of God, fell upon Saul, the tentmaker of Tarsus—Roman citizen, Greek scholar, Hebrew patriot, religious zealot, flaming evangelist, and profound theologian.

Hence, next to understanding Jesus, it is necessary for the modern Christian to know Paul, through whose mind the

27016

Gospel of Jesus has been filtered. To Sholem Asch, the novelist, we are indebted for a revealing portrait, which in accuracy of detail will probably not be duplicated in our generation, if ever. But even so satisfactory and reverent a book as *The Apostle* leaves room for an appraisal of the mind of Paul: its logic, its profundity, and its versatility.

It is for this purpose of drawing the curtains aside and allowing us to watch the mind of Paul at work, that Chester Warren Quimby, whose gifted and scholarly pen has already demonstrated his ability to recreate the great characters of our holy faith, has prepared for us *Paul for Everyone*. As one of the staff of writers for *The Christian Advocate*, whose articles on scripture interpretation have won wide approval, we take pride in this extended work. Having watched Mr. Quimby producing material for several years, we believe this is his best.

The reverent student will read these pages and exclaim again and again, "Why, of course! I never saw it before, but it's true! That explains it!" And out of the reading he will come with a sense of profound gratitude for the author, who has actually ushered him into the presence of the great Christian. There is a great spiritual adventure ahead for the reader of these pages.

ROY L. SMITH
Editor, "The Christian Advocate"

THE IMPORTANCE OF PAUL

"More abundantly than they all"

We do well to give heed to Paul. Five times in Christian history our faith has leaped as a fire, illuminating the world and igniting the souls of men. Each time the kindling spark has come from this Master Apostle.

The first conflagration was fired by Paul himself. In a few short years of burning zeal he planted the gospel torch in the chief cities of the northeastern Mediterranean, from Syrian Antioch to Rome. The next kindling came four hundred years later, when Augustine, soiled in soul, troubled in mind and weary with searching, chanced upon Paul's words in the Epistle of *Romans*, "Put ye on the Lord Jesus Christ, and make not provision for the flesh, to fulfil the lusts thereof." Then and there Augustine surrendered to Paul's Lord and Master. Then and there began the arduous service in the days of tottering Rome which established in a faltering generation an unshakable faith in the abiding City of God.

Eleven hundred years later the smoldering Christian torch once more blazed forth as a beacon. Into Martin Luther's soul burned Paul's words from *Galatians*, "The righteous shall live by faith," and Luther went out to initiate the Protestant Reformation, opening the door for every man to be priest and king before God through Christ.

The third advance came two hundred years later, when

John Wesley, hearing one reading from Luther's *Preface to the Epistle to the Romans*, felt his heart strangely warmed. That strange warming became the spreading fire of the Evangelical Revival.

In our own day it was Paul again, who came at the close of World War I as a candle of the Lord to a discouraged Swiss pastor, and made him a shining light of the Eternal. Karl Barth's book, *A Commentary on the Romans*, fanned the complacent embers of an easy-going liberalism into a blazing fervor for the Divine Sovereignty.

This is the astonishing record of Paul. In him and his letters lies an inexhaustible power to startle a somnolent faith from its sleep. Next to our Lord, we do well to give ear to Paul.

It is for this reason that I have long wanted to write a book on "Paul for Everyone." For Paul is difficult to know. The New Testament material about him is scattered through at least ten books. In them the facts concerning him often are concealed in matters only indirectly connected with him, or they lie buried in outmoded first-century thought and custom. Study alone can dig out and correlate the data needed to expose the Great Apostle in the fullness of his might. Neither his life nor letters are lounge-chair reading. Though Paul is for everyone, and not for the brilliant scholar only, he does require hard thought. The digging is often difficult, but once Paul is discovered acquaintance with him will revolutionize the prospector's soul.

The form this book takes grows out of long experience. Years ago as a cub professor, when first preparing to teach Paul, I said: "The way is plain. I have only to work out the established facts of Paul's career from *The Acts*, supplement these with others derived from his letters, and add his main ideas as outlined in his epistles. Then I shall have Paul alive, his career and thought complete." But, alas! the vital facts of his career and the profound principles of his faith do not, for the great part, appear in the main points of *The Acts* and the outline of his letters. The real Paul still eluded me.

Years later it became my task to teach young preachers their ABC's of Paul. The assigned text attempted to elucidate Paul in the conventional surface fashion I had so fallaciously tried. Having perused the text, the young preachers had learned little of importance about Paul. "I want," I said, "some way to teach Paul that will explore his whole life in a plain full-rounded fashion." The result is the plan embodied in this book, and outlined in its Table of Contents.

This treatment of Paul's personality, religious experience, journeys, career, letters, world view, Gospel, and achievements as a unified whole on an introductory level for Everyone is the most and perhaps the only original attribute of this volume. Most works on Paul follow well established, conventional lines. Some review his life according to *The Acts*, fitting in the facts about his letters. Others put the chief emphasis upon his thought and letters, adding such items about his career and character as seem needed. The third class deals with some special aspect of his life or writings. Few, if any, attempt to give a well-rounded introduction embodying all the main phases of the Great Apostle. This is the purpose of this volume. It seeks to present as complete and vivid a portrait as a single, simple work will permit of "Paul for Everyone."

CONTENTS

xiii

Chapter 1

THE TORMENTED PERSECUTOR

BEFORE THE DAMASCUS ROAD

"Who shall deliver me out of the body of this death?"

THE FIRST TIME we meet Paul, called by his Hebrew name of Saul, he is represented as standing to one side watching a gruesome spectacle. Just outside Jerusalem's walls near the Temple area, a mob is milling in fury. It is composed of the High Priest, members of the Sanhedrin, officials of the Temple, and the unruly rabble that always gathers where excitement calls. The chief priests and their immediate attendants have cast aside their outer garments to make aiming more accurate and throwing more powerful. Shouting invectives, they hurl heavy stones upon a bruised and bleeding man. This man, Stephen, an outstanding Christian leader, suddenly straightens himself upon his knees, lifts his face toward heaven, and cries aloud, "Lord Jesus, receive my spirit." Smitten down, he again lifts himself to speak one last prayer, "Lord, lay not this sin to their charge." Then he collapses and dies.

All this while the young Paul is standing by, keeping guard over the stoners' garments. Upon the brutal stoning he looks with sympathetic approval. Stephen is getting exactly the execution ordered by the law of Moses for all blasphemers. So there Paul stands, in unquestioning righteousness "consenting unto his death." The record continues: "And there arose on that day a great persecution against the church which was in Jerusalem; and they were all scattered abroad. . . . But Saul laid waste the church, entering into every house, and dragging men and women committed them to prison."

Such is our terrible introduction to Paul, the zealous, fanatical, cruel persecutor. An ugly picture, yet one exciting curiosity. Who was Paul?

Physically, Paul was unimpressive. Ancient tradition has pictured him as short, stocky, bow-legged, with piercing eyes under meeting eyebrows. He had a large, hooked nose, and later in life, if not now, he was bald-headed. When earning his living by his trade, his hands were black-stained from tent weaving. His movements were quick and graceful, and he was a ready talker.

This, it should be noted, is only tradition. It does not come from any sure authority, although it adds up to a possible and reasonable portrait. Certain elements in it appear to be authentic. That his movements were quick is verified by the record of *The Acts*, that as he rose to speak Paul customarily "stretched forth his hand." To gain attention, he began gesticulating before he spoke. As to ready talking, preaching the Gospel [1] was his business. On one occasion, at least, he "prolonged his speech until midnight." He probably possessed the sharp, bright eye of the very intelligent. Many a man in the Aegean cities must have experienced the hypnotic gaze which Elymas felt when Paul "fastened his eyes on him." His general unimpressive presence is attested by the Corinthian taunt, "his bodily presence is weak."

Except for the scars received from the stonings and

[1] For reasons for capitalizing the Gospel see under *Gospel*, page 170.

2

scourgings of his later journeys so that he could testify, "I bear branded on my body the marks of Jesus," this is all we can ever know of Paul's physical appearance. The only other fact we have about his body concerns his health.

Paul suffered from an incurable malady. Whether it began tormenting him in these days of his young manhood we cannot know. In later years it hung over him as a crippling menace. Every type of both wild and plausible guess has been made as to its nature: malaria, epilepsy, inflamed eyes so common in the orient, neurasthenia, insomnia, migraine, palsy and a dozen more. They are all guesses, depending upon infinitesimal evidence. Why we cannot make even a plausible diagnosis of Paul's ailment is plain. Paul never breathed a definite hint about it. He gave but two descriptions of it, neither of them medical: "a messenger of Satan to buffet me," and "a thorn in the flesh."

Though we cannot so much as guess the name of his disease, we do get glimpses of its effect. It afflicted him in Galatia, and he was ill later when he first entered Corinth, as he once reminded the Corinthian church: "I was with you in weakness." It disrupted his plans, compelling him to make unexpected changes, even to sending him where he apparently had had no intention of going. So he reminds his Galatian converts, "Ye know that because of an infirmity of the flesh I preached the gospel unto you the first time." Also, it seems to have taken some outward form humiliating to him, and exciting aversion in others. For he continues, "That which was a temptation to you in my flesh ye despised not, nor rejected." That it was also extremely painful is probable from his describing his complaint as "a thorn in the flesh." It was so disabling that he was compelled, apparently, to take Luke, the physician, along with him, at least part of the time. That may not

3

have been Luke's only reason for accompanying him, but as *The Acts* suggests and Paul's letters show, the good doctor was often his traveling companion.

If medical aid was unavailing, so also was prayer. "I besought the Lord thrice, that it might depart from me." The only relief he received was the divine assurance, "My grace is sufficient for thee."

In spite of this "thorn in the flesh," Paul's energy was enormous. He was extraordinarily tough. The statement of *The Acts* that Paul "laid waste the church" with such strength-demanding verbs as "entering every house," and "dragging men and women," is an evidence not only of his youthful fury, but also of his vitality. The statement that a little later Paul was "yet breathing threatening and slaughter" is added evidence of his restless activity.

There is a true distinction between an infirmity and energy. Though Paul suffered from an incurable malady, his energy was exhaustless. Here we see it in the fury of destructive persecution. Later it became his unceasing asset. He could float on a spar "a night and a day . . . in the deep." He could be stoned and left for dead, but on the following day journey on to the next city. He could write of his work, as compared with others more in health than himself as, "in labors more abundantly." He could travel, preach, earn his living, attend to the affairs of his scattered churches, write letters, survive shipwrecks, stonings, imprisonments, hunger, cold, and scourgings. His recuperative powers were enormous.

Paul had a further explanation for his unquenchable energy. His surprising vigor was not only natural, it was divinely maintained. "And he hath said unto me," Paul witnessed, "My grace is sufficient for thee: for my power is made perfect in weakness."

4

Paul's energy, ailment and swiftness of gesture would lead one to expect him to be high-strung and hot-tempered. A youth who could take satisfaction in execution by stoning, lay waste the church, enter every house, drag forth men and women, and lash out in threatening and slaughter, call a member of the Sanhedrin, "Thou whited wall," and write the blazing *Galatians*, is a person of taut temperament. In such a physique are seething volcanic emotions capable of sustaining tireless zeal and indomitable courage.

Such was the physical make-up of this potential apostle. One gets the impression of a little man hurrying along, too unimpressive to command a second glance until some quick movement, augmented by a speedy word and backed by a gleaming eye, would shackle the attention. "Weak" in appearance, yet fascinating the attention; doomed to an inevitable chronic disorder yet exhaustless in energy; nervous and hot-tempered yet controlled by constant self-buffetings; this is the paradoxical man whose heroic career has never been exceeded.

Culturally Paul was cosmopolitan. Born a Jew, he was according to the Law "circumcised the eighth day, of the stock of Israel, of the tribe of Benjamin, a Hebrew of Hebrews; as touching the law, a Pharisee; as touching zeal, persecuting the church; as touching the righteousness which is in the law, found blameless." None could be more Jewish than that. The tribe of Benjamin was one of two not carried away captive with the destruction of Samaria and lost among the nations. In Paul, so he proudly wrote, beat the blood of Abraham in pristine purity. This little tribe had given Israel her first king, the commanding and tragic Saul. After him Paul had been named. His Pharisaism represented the faith of his fathers in its strictest observance

5

and its most rigid refusal to compromise with gentile influences. Of this almost super-Jewishness, Paul was rightly proud. In after years when certain of his opponents tried to undermine him, casting aspersions upon his Jewish loyalty and accusing him of looseness toward the exactions of the Mosaic Law, he hotly replied, "Are they Hebrews? so am I. Are they Israelites? so am I. Are they the seed of Abraham? so am I." "I advanced in the Jews' religion beyond many of mine own age among my countrymen being more exceedingly zealous for the traditions of my fathers." It was this abounding patriotic Jewish loyalty that fanned his persecuting fervor into flame. Jesus' followers, he believed, were traitors to the Law.

Who Paul's father and mother were is unknown. No hint of them has come down to us from the New Testament or elsewhere. Of the rest of his family we know nothing, except of one sister. We come upon her years later in Jerusalem, after his final arrest. She was married, and had at least one well-grown son. She evidently moved in high circles close to the great Sanhedrin. For this nephew of Paul's picked up knowledge of its secret plottings to assassinate Paul, and gave warning. Somehow the sister was sympathetic enough with the followers of The Way to be loyal to her brother, yet sufficiently orthodox to keep her high connections. To this Paul owed the sparing of his life.

Though this is all we can ever know of Paul's family, we can be sure of its intense devotion to the practices of the Jewish faith. In his pious home and in the local synagogue, he plainly received an emphatic religious training. As Paul's later writings show, from his early years he was deeply versed in the Septuagint (LXX)—the Greek version of his Hebrew Bible. He knew the Law of God.

Like all Jews of his day, he was skilled in a handicraft.

He could earn his living with his hands. Notable rabbis of the time were millers, shoemakers, tailors, bakers and potters. A trade, they said, kept one from robbery. It put temptation to wrongdoing out of mind. Paul was a tentmaker. By it he supported himself, and even his companions, through his missionary years. "Ye yourselves know that these hands ministered unto my necessities, and to them that were with me." "Am I not an apostle? . . . Have we no right to eat and to drink? . . . have we not a right to forbear working? . . . Nevertheless we did not use this right; but we bear all things, that we may cause no hindrance to the gospel of Christ." All his life, by his tent-weaving or similar work, Paul paid his own way.

Whether Paul was a widower, or whether he ever married we can never be sure. In *The Acts* there is no suggestion of his having a wife. He certainly had none with him on his missionary journeys, for he wrote the Corinthian church, "Have we no right to lead about a wife that is a believer, even as the rest of the apostles, and the brethren of the Lord, and Cephas?" Evidently others were accompanied by their wives, but he enjoyed no such comforting companionship, for he adds, "But I say to the unmarried and to widows, It is good for them if they abide even as I." Whether this implies that he was always a bachelor, or was now a widower cannot be ascertained. Bachelors had no standing in Judaism, yet in his early Jerusalem years Paul stood in high Jewish esteem. Members of the Sanhedrin had to be married. While Paul stood close to the Sanhedrin, and the Sanhedrin entrusted him with important powers, it is not certain that he was a member of that body. His youthfulness would seem to preclude it. Hence both his precise relation to the Sanhedrin and his exact marital status cannot now definitely be determined.

The one central certainty about Paul, the Jew, is his fixed loyalty to the Law. This fanatical devotion must have begun in his very early years. His transfer from his native Tarsus could but intensify it. The sharp change from the restless, easy-going Greek city to the barren, rocky knoll of Jerusalem could but increase his Jewish patriotism. There was the Temple, and there were the many synagogues scattered about the sacred city. Visiting Jews from all over the Roman world crowded into Jerusalem at Passover time. There Paul's Cilician comrades maintained their own house of worship. Thus the young student eager to enrich his knowledge of the Law came into contact with the intense zeal of world-wide Jewry.

At the Temple school where he studied, Paul sat at the feet of the great liberal rabbi, Gamaliel. Years later to the mob howling for his blood, he pointed with pride to his days under the learned master of the Law, "I am a Jew, . . . brought up in this city, at the feet of Gamaliel." It was here his knowledge of and zeal for the Law were perfected.

It was in this zeal for the Law that his satisfaction over Stephen's death was rooted. A vigorous and dangerous enemy of orthodoxy was being liquidated. Later in his Christian years, Paul never lost his Jewish loyalty. He still boasted that he was a "Hebrew of Hebrews." To the end he longed to be reunited with his Jewish compatriots in the bond of Christian fellowship. His deepest desire was their acceptance of the Gospel. To accomplish that he would gladly give his life. "For I could wish that I myself were anathema from Christ for my brethren's sake, my kinsmen according to the flesh: who are Israelites; whose is the adoption, and the glory, and the covenants, and the giving of the law, and the service of God, and the promises; whose are the fathers, and of whom is Christ as concerning the flesh." Jewish patriotism could go no higher.

Next as a cosmopolitan, Paul was a Greek. His native city, Tarsus in Cilicia in Asia Minor, was a Greek-speaking gentile city. A port city, a university town, a trading outlet for the fertile Cilician plain, Tarsus was in Paul's day one of the great urban centers of the world. Here was wealth, culture, a richly varied population, and at the near-by waterfront, the tug of far places. It was a city that excited one's pride, and Paul never lost his pride in it. To the officer who finally arrested him, Paul quite properly boasted, "I am a Jew, of Tarsus in Cilicia, a citizen of no mean city."

How deeply the free Greek life of the city influenced his boyhood cannot be guessed. It is a pleasant fancy to picture that bright Jewish boy as playing about the waterfront docks and dreaming of distant ports; or romping about the university, mingling with students from the world over and picking up bits of higher learning and scraps of academic jargon, of mingling with gentile boys in the street, and even peeking into pagan temples, thus rubbing off the sharp corners of his Jewish exclusiveness. But all this is pure fancy. That Jewish life in Tarsus was broader than in Jerusalem goes without argument. That his daily speech was Greek, not Hebrew, and his scriptures the Greek Septuagint is evidenced by his later letters. But life in the Jewish quarter was still strictly Jewish. It abhorred all things gentile: temples, idols, homes and "unclean" foods. Business relations with gentiles were inevitable, but social relations were sharply limited. Food restrictions of the Mosaic law cut them shorter. Stern Hebrew morals curtailed them further. Attendance at the synagogue school confined them to yet tighter limits. In later years Paul boasted not of his liberal ways in a lax gentile city, but of his stern Jewish exclusive-

9

ness. Always he had been a "Hebrew of Hebrews." Paul was from first to last a Jew of Jews.

The true meaning of Tarsus for the growing Paul seems to have lain in two directions. First, he was city bred and trained. It was cities he knew and understood. It was cities in which he later wrought his mighty works. While Paul's use of rural terms is more frequent than is commonly supposed, they have not the full-bodied richness of the country-bred Man of Nazareth. Paul was urban. In gentile Tarsus, also, the Greek language gave Paul a ready understanding of the non-Jewish world, quite impossible, for example, to the Galilean, Aramaic-speaking Peter. The free Greek gentile world was native air to Paul.

Finally, as a cosmopolitan, Paul was a Roman citizen. Originally Roman citizenship granted special privileges to non-Latin citizens of the Empire in recognition of outstanding merit. It conferred such benefits as exemption from death by crucifixion, and gave the right of appeal to the Emperior's tribunal. In time Roman citizenship could be bought. The chief captain at Paul's final arrest declared, "With a great sum obtained I this citizenship." It also became an inherited right. With justifiable pride Paul answered the chief captain, "But I am a Roman born." Whether his family first obtained Roman citizenship by merit or by purchase cannot now be learned.

Paul customarily insisted upon his full citizenship rights. After his arrest, scourging and incarceration at Philippi, and with release at hand, Paul stood upon his Roman rights. "They have beaten us publicly, uncondemned, men that are Romans, and have cast us into prison; and do they now cast us out privily? Nay verily; but let them come themselves and bring us out." Proud as he was of his pure Jewish blood, straight from the ancient tribe of Benjamin and the distant days of King Saul, Paul was equally jealous of his inherited honor of full citizenship in the world-wide Roman Empire.

Such was Paul, the cosmopolitan. Of course he had not yet flowered into the fullness of grace so characteristic of his mature Christian mission. From the beginning the seeds of world citizenship lay in him. A strict Jew, a proud Roman, a Greek sympathizer, reared in a flourishing gentile city of wealth, culture and wide horizons, and educated at the intense center of all Judaism, he had in him the roots of a world outlook. Roman by birth, Greek by environment, and Jewish by religion, he harbored a universal mind. A Jew with gentile sympathies and a Roman citizen enthralled by the Empire, he later set himself to capture Jew, Greek, Roman, and the Empire itself for his Lord and Christ. Beyond all others he could say, "I am become all things to all men, that I may by all means save some."

Religiously Paul was unhappy. His experience with the Law, instead of bringing him rich satisfaction left him restless, impotent, conscience-stricken and dismayed. For a man consumed by intense zeal, possessed of acute moral insight, subject to volcanic emotions, and living "in all good conscience" in the Law, this deep failure of his faith to bring him abiding peace and joy was tragedy indeed. Later in life he described the tortured struggle of his soul. *Romans* 7 is almost universally accepted as Paul's description of his own disheartening battle with the Law.

"Howbeit, I had not known sin, except through the law: for I had not known coveting, except the law had said, Thou shalt not covet. . . . And I was alive apart from the law once: but when the commandment came, sin revived, and I died; and the commandment, which was unto life,

11

this I found to be unto death: for sin, finding occasion, through the commandment beguiled me, and through it slew me." "I died . . . it slew me." Terrible words of a terrible religious disaster.

This may hint at some otherwise hidden boyhood tragedy. Something of what may have happened can be illustrated from a youthful experience of Augustine. Augustine's spiritual disaster came in part from stealing pears. 'Yet I lusted to thieve, and did it, compelled by no hunger, nor poverty, but through a cloyedness of welldoing, and a pamperedness of iniquity. For I stole that, of which I had enough, and much better. Nor cared I to enjoy what I stole, but joyed in the theft and sin itself. A pear tree there was near our vineyard, laden with fruit, tempting neither for colour nor taste. To shake and rob this, some lewd young fellows of us went, late one night, (having according to our pestilent custom prolonged our sports in the streets till then,) and took huge loads, not for our eating, but to fling to the very hogs, having only tasted them. And this, but to do, what we liked only, because it was misliked.' [2]

This causes us to chuckle. A typical boyish escapade! 'Swiping' fruit for the thrill of the mild risk involved! Robbing orchards to gain the exciting censure of being dubbed 'toughs.' In later life we would not consider such childhood roguery worth a passing regret. We would classify it as part of growing up. But not so Augustine. Decades later

[2] The Confessions of St. Augustine, Bk. II, [IV] 9, pp. 25–26. Translated by E. B. Pusey, D.D., Everyman's Library, E. P. Dutton & Co., New York. Of course there was much more than this in Augustine's troubled moral life, but this pear-stealing seems to have aroused his sense of moral helplessness, and to have remained with him as a continuing, haunting experience.

it haunted him. For him the stolen pears were a moral crisis. They symbolized the arrival of conscious power to know and choose right from wrong, *and a moral inability to do aught but the wrong.* He startlingly realized he could never be his own moral master. It is a universal experience.[3]

Possibly it is some such boyhood prank as this to which Paul refers. There was the Law with its fixed standards. As a growing child he was little conscious of any personal responsibility to them. Then for the first time, busy at some youngster's activity, he became conscious of a clear choice. Almost certainly, like Augustine's pears, it was no great wickedness. But like Augustine's petty theft, it held eternal moral consequences for Paul. Like Augustine and like ourselves, Paul did the wrong. With a sharp shock he knew that his moral life was beyond his ability to control. Some inner gleaming light went black. "Sin revived, and I died . . . for sin . . . slew me." As with Augustine, it remained for Paul a continuing experience. Never again, for all the tutelage of the Law, would he be his moral master. "For to will [the good] is present with me, but to do that which is good is not. For the good which I would I do not; but the evil which I would not, that I practice. . . . To me who would do good, evil is present. . . . Wretched man that I am! who shall deliver me out of the body of this death?" Thus the Law, which was his standard of high practice, and from which he expected salvation, galled his freedom, convicted his innocence, quenched his power, and denied him

[3] John Woolman tells how as "a little boy" he, by throwing stones, killed a mother bird and "was seized with horror and remorse." Having a more placid disposition and more normal religious development than either Paul or Augustine, this experience does not seem to have been so critical with him. But that it burned in his memory not less than a quarter of a century later is significant. Like Paul, Augustine, and all earnest youthful souls, he found his moral life beyond his power to manage. See *John Woolman,* by Janet Whitney, Little, Brown & Co., 1942, pp. 28–30 and 41–45.

peace. Keeping the Law with all Pharisaic meticulousness brought him no quieting forgiveness and no restoring sense of divine fellowship. A terrible taskmaster, it held him its impotent slave.

In all this zeal for the Law Paul was utterly sincere. When we first meet him, this diligence is manifesting itself in approving Stephen's violent death, and dragging other Christians to prison. Such vigorous activity might be attributed to a desire to win favor with superiors, secure quicker recognition, and obtain swifter promotion. Zeal may indeed be born of self-interest, but hardly of hypocrisy. Paul's alarm at Christian propaganda and success was genuine. The Galilean followers of the Crucified Criminal were saying that the Revolutionary Felon had risen from the dead, that the Unkingly Heretic was the promised Messiah, that the Condemned Convict was the true Saviour, and the Executed Malefactor took precedence over Moses. Blasphemy! As the Mosaic Law specified, these propagandists must be rounded up and stoned. Not to do so would be an act of insincerity. In later time Paul readily admitted his shortcomings—a persecutor of the saints and a religious failure in keeping the Law. But he never admitted any insincerity. He honestly thought he had been right. Before hostile judges he dared bluntly assert, "Brethren, I have lived before God in all good conscience until this day."

Whether Paul had ever seen the earthly Jesus must remain undetermined. All his own references to the matter are ambiguous. And there are no others. Once he wrote the Corinthians, "Have I not seen Jesus our Lord?" But he may be referring to his vision of the Risen Christ on the Damascus Road. This is the only possible meaning of his later word, "And last of all, as to the child untimely born, he appeared to me also." Only one other time does he men-

14

tion the matter. "Even though we have known Christ after the flesh, yet now we know him so no more." Whatever the statement may mean, it does not definitely and without equivocation say, "I did know Jesus in the flesh." However, whether Paul actually once knew the earthly Jesus, it is certain that in his letters he made no direct use of any such knowledge. For Paul, the Christian, Jesus was forever the Risen Lord.

But without question Paul did possess an intimate knowledge of Jesus' earthly career. His letters contain many touches that can be explained only on the premise of such a knowledge. He early spent two weeks in Jerusalem with Peter, and James, Jesus' own brother. One can pick up a large amount of knowledge in "fifteen days." For it is not to be supposed that they talked about the weather! Furthermore, Paul must have learned much about Jesus while he was making havoc in the church. Unless we are to suppose that he nabbed his victims on mere suspicion, and threw them into prison untried, we can only conclude that as he spied on their meetings, "entering into every house," he heard their testimonies, their stories of Jesus' deeds, and their rehearsals of his teachings. Along with their tales of Jesus went their new understanding of the scripture. There, in the Law itself, they found indisputable evidence that this despised teacher was really the true Messiah. To Paul it must have been new, crazy, but often impossible to refute.

So little by little, a bit here and another there, Paul gathered a considerable store of facts, incidents, deeds and sayings of the Crucified Carpenter. The more he heard, the more violent Paul became. This unseemly Galilean had strangely enough spent his time in deeds of gentle mercy, but in his name his followers were undermining the Law of Moses. They must be obliterated.

Finally, Paul had seen men suffer for Jesus. With steadfast courage and with confident prayer they endured without flinching. Exactly how this beauty in tragedy at first affected the youthful Paul is not known. He never again directly referred to it. But later, did the quiet, serene heroism of the Believers begin to haunt him? We know he never was able to shake off the cruelties he inflicted upon the saints. "For I am the least of the apostles, that am not meet to be called an apostle, because I persecuted the church of God." Thus, paradoxically, his cruel persecutions became the first step of his Bethel road up to his vision of God in Christ.

Could we have followed Paul through the months of his persecuting fury, we would not have suspected that this eager defender of the faith carried a hungry and aching heart, a disquiet conscience, and deep misgivings of mind. The followers of The Way had plainly found a forgiveness, joy, peace, fellowship and victory for which Paul suffered a thirst he could never slake. Instead of calling God (as he did) the eternal Jahweh, they knew him intimately as "Abba," Father. He was putting to death those who possessed that for which he longed, the Law could not give, and he could not find. He was hounding those who followed One they called "Lord," and whose testimony revealed that he did no evil among men, but went about doing good. And so many of their arguments from the scriptures Paul could not, with all his skill, rebut. Could it be that he was wrong? "Wretched man that I am! who shall deliver me out of the body of this death?"

Chapter 2

THE BELATED CONVERT

On the Damascus Road

"It was the good pleasure of God . . . to reveal his Son in me."

THE SECOND TIME we meet Paul considerable time has elapsed. Much has happened. Paul's laying waste the church did not result, as he had expected, in its destruction. To his dismay it furthered its expansion. The Christians, driven from Jerusalem, "were all scattered abroad throughout the regions of Judaea and Samaria." And as they were scattered abroad, they "went about preaching the word." Soon there was no longer just one company of Christians in Jerusalem.[1] There were many little bands of believers spread among the Judaean and Samaritan villages. By kicking into the fire Paul had not stamped it out. Instead he had kindled many new fires. Eventually word drifted back to Jerusalem that there was a Christian community in far-off Damascus, some one hundred and forty air miles to the northeast, a great distance in that day of slow travel.

The news that in Damascus a group of Christians was flourishing unmolested, greatly increased his alarm. So, still "breathing threatening and slaughter against the disciples of the Lord," Paul "went to the high priest, and

[1] *The Acts* is plainly a condensed, summary account. It is not to be supposed that after Pentecost every last follower of Jesus was concentrated in Jerusalem. Galilee must have had many groups of The Way, that quickly became a part of the church.

17

asked letters of him to Damascus unto the synagogues, that if he found any that were of The Way, whether men or women, he might bring them bound to Jerusalem."

Armed with the authority of these letters Paul set out for Damascus. Unless he traveled by swift racing camel, it was at least a week's travel to the Syrian city. After the seething, hectic days in Jerusalem, this slow, silent journey brought Paul long hours of meditation. But in his soul there was no tranquility. Within him his futile efforts to keep the Law fought in desperate conflict with his knowledge of the Christians' inner joy and peace. Could he ever possess what they so radiantly manifested, except he too surrender to The Way?

It was hard for Paul to turn Christian. The spectacular nature of his conversion is proof of his severe struggle. Such dramatic experiences come only through sharp psychological conflict. The reasons for this stern spiritual battle are fairly clear.

To desert the Law for The Way and accept an unkingly Messiah was counter to all Paul's training and beliefs. The Mosaic Law had been divinely given. Israel was God's chosen people. The Law was his holy covenant with them. For disobedience to this Law the nation had suffered calamities of pestilence and earthquake, invasions and captivity. To desert the Law would be for Paul to deny God, scorn the covenant, flout his family, affront his friends, and spurn the divine history of his nation. No devout and patriotic Jew could be so despicable. Besides, the Law set forth the highest religion men knew. "Hear, O Israel, the Lord our God is One: and thou shalt love the Lord thy God with all thy heart, and with all thy soul, and with all thy might." Nothing that Paul as a boy had seen in the streets of gentile

18

Tarsus had approached such excellence. No other religion was as exalted.

To yield was against Paul's deepest principles. To turn Christian now would sicken his parents, dishonor the home friends, surrender his future, break the Law and deny his God. That would be treason to himself, his fellows and his God. He owed them everything by way of inheritance, training, practical help and the Truth. All were expecting great things of him. Now they were entrusting him with the crucial responsibility of stamping out this insidious threat to the Law and Judaism. The attack was from within the ranks. These followers of The Way counted themselves as good Jews. They were circumcised keepers of the Law. They attended the regular synagogue and Temple services. Had they been idolatrous gentiles there would be no danger. But these iniquitous people were perverting the very scriptures to prove that The Way was the true fulfillment of the Law! Thus they made themselves out to be better than other Jews. In them the covenant of God had come to perfection! Wolves in sheep's clothing, appearing as angels of light, they deceived and led astray many well-meaning but misguided sons of Abraham. Against the invidious serpent within, Paul had been given full authority to smite. The Jerusalem officials were relying upon him to annihilate this blasphemous heresy. To desert them now would be base ingratitude, vilest treason. Such Paul could never be. Above all else he honored and clung to his friends. Later, as a Christian, in his letters he mentions some fifty friends by name, sending them greetings, commending them to other friends, giving information concerning them. Paul leaned on his friends. By turning Christian now, he would cut himself off from them, and brand himself in their eyes and his own, a turncoat.

19

To do so would invite hardship and suffering: If he entered The Way, he, too, would be persecuted. And he knew the horrors that meant. All the agonies he had inflicted upon others would be doubled against him. He would be hated as a person far more evil than the misguided followers of the Galilean impostor. He would be despised as the betrayer of a trust, and a deserter of the faith. He could not safely remain in Jerusalem, and he might not dare return to Tarsus. His only security would be to flee into exile. He had stood by, approving Stephen's stoning. He could hardly expect an easier fate. Instead of a long, useful life, coming down to old age ripe in years, rich in dignity and laden with honors, his would be the short life and sudden death of a traitor.

How many, if any, of these items filled Paul's mind in his restless days before he started for Damascus we cannot know. Certainly each of these issues was there to be faced. As a brilliant youth, unhappy in his religion, longing for satisfaction of spirit, acquainted with the courage and joy of many Christians, it is impossible to believe these factors did not, in some form, focus acutely in his keen mind. Not as in this cool, analytical outline to be sure, but in some hot, burning clarity. He wanted what the Christians possessed, but the price was great. How could he forsake the divine law, surrender his ambition, desert his friends, and espouse the suffering? Thus hard was it for Paul to turn Christian!

With such a conflict raging in his soul, Paul set out for distant Damascus. Except for an occasional word with his companions, and the click of his donkey's feet against the stones in the path, all was quiet. The noise and turmoil of Jerusalem were left behind. In the long silence of the days, during the slow travel, Paul had time to collect and steady himself. Some such thoughts as these presumably raced through his mind: 'This movement grows. The more I persecute it, the more it flourishes. Once it was centered in Jerusalem. Now it spreads like fire in a field. It rages throughout Judea. It has leaped into Samaria. It burns brightly in Galilee. Now it has lit its torch in distant Damascus. The harder I toil, the faster it expands. Why? Stephen died not like a sinner, but like a saint. The yoke of the Law is a burden wearisome to men. It brings me not peace and power, but defeat and slavery. I wage a losing fight. Can this Jesus truly be the Christ?' So day after silent day, Paul rode on with questions seething in his mind and doubts battling in his soul.

Then one day, over the horizon, the roof tops of Damascus hove in sight. The final crisis had come. To go on and fulfill his commission would mean he had chosen to abide in the Law, taskmaster though it was. If he turned back, The Way would grow and grow unmolested into—what? If he surrendered to The Way, could peace of heart and liberty of spirit be his also? His spiritual fever had reached its crisis. He could battle no more.

There on the stony plain outside Damascus, God gave Paul some great, clarifying, satisfying vision of the risen Jesus that answered all his racking questions. Paul "saw" and was at peace. "It was the good pleasure of God . . . through his grace, to reveal his Son in me." "And last of all, as to the child untimely born, he appeared to me also." Stunned, his mind in chaos, too bewildered to eat or drink, his taut body suddenly unstrung, Paul lay in a stupor. He who had expected to enter Damascus with power and leave it with glory, was now lifted up and supported into the city

21

on the arms of his friends. He needed rest, friendship and counsel.

Word got about the city that Paul had arrived. With the rumor probably went the word that he was ill. The trembling band of Christians found their danger temporarily averted. Perhaps God might yet save them. One of their number, Ananias by name, had evidently prayed over the matter. News of Paul's supposed illness filled him with concern. Was the arch persecutor working a ruse, or might he be suffering not a disease of the body, but sickness of soul? After some hesitant delay, and with much dread, but moved irresistibly by the divine Spirit, Ananias sought out the young zealot. Under his kindly ministrations Paul's perplexities suddenly clarified. Joyously he felt himself "filled with the Holy Spirit." He knew in whom he believed. For the first time in his religious maturity, he experienced peace and liberty, power, joy and divine fellowship. Back at once to normal, he sat up and asked for something to eat.

Immediately he felt the impulse to proclaim the Good News to the gentile world. But he did not yet feel himself to be ready. For, as he says in *Galatians*, "straightway . . . I went away into Arabia." Just why he does not say. Apparently, he must first fathom and clarify his joyous experience, relate its significance to the Scriptures, and form it into a convincing message. Like his Master in the Wilderness, he needed to adjust himself to the blinding vision he had received, and see all things clearly in its revealing light.

How came Paul to receive this vision, and how arc its details to be explained? Visions do not come out of the blue, but result from tense psychological conflict. The first element that made possible Paul's vision was his utter sincerity. However wrongheaded he was, Paul was wholly honest. "I have lived before God in all good conscience." Next, he put his convictions into action. "After the straitest sect of our religion I lived a Pharisee." He tried to live out the Law to its last jot and tittle. Gamaliel, the great Jewish teacher, who played a "wait-see" policy, never came to any vision of Christ. But sincerity, put into action, is a straight, if sometimes arduous road to God. Then, Paul's failure to find peace in the Law led him to deep searchings of heart. And finally, the courageous joy of the Christians who prospered under his persecutions upset his certainties. After all, they did no evil deeds. Were they really wicked? With these elements centered in his mind, Paul was mentally set to receive a vision. All he needed was the quiet afforded him along the Damascus Road.

Of the actual experience Paul, himself, gives us no details. Only twice in his letters does he directly refer to it. Each time he gives no description of the outward occurrences, but confines himself to its inner meaning. God did "reveal his Son in me," and Christ "appeared to me also."

It is only from *The Acts* that we get picturesque details. And they are not to be taken as literal history. No crisis of the soul can be expressed in cold mathematical formulae. Only figurative language can give hints of the true inner experience that outruns the power of words fully to describe. And figurative language must never be turned into dull prose.

Paul's vision before Damascus can never be fully explained in scientific terms and psychological analysis. One cannot say that because Paul fell to the ground under a great light, he was struck by lightning. Men have been so struck and temporarily blinded and paralyzed. But we do not know that a thunderstorm was raging just when Paul collapsed. Besides, lightning bolts, whatever their physical effects, do not have the power to transform a bewildered, cruel fanatic into a constructive, heroic saint. Nor will it do to say that Paul suffered a sunstroke. We do not know that the day was bright and the sun hot. For all we know it was a cloudy day in the dead of icy winter. Moreover, sunstroke, however benumbing to the body, has no power in itself to convert a convinced Pharisee into a disciple of the Lord Jesus. For the writer of *The Acts* it was a *miraculous light* never seen on land or sea.

No conversion, much less Paul's, can ever be fully explained, for more than human factors are involved. The Spirit of God enters as a divine invasion. And the workings of the divine Spirit cannot be analyzed in a test tube or investigated by a psychological questionnaire. The dazzling light, the heavenly voice, the mysterious blindness, and the physical collapse are colors painting a brilliant picture of an exhausted man, at war with his own spiritual questions, receiving the saving grace of God.

Paul's own explanation is all we need, for his later life bore it out. On the Damascus Road Jesus revealed himself to Paul. Jesus, once crucified, dead and buried, was alive! He was risen from the dead. He was God's Anointed One. Peace of heart, joy of soul, liberty of spirit and fellowship with the Father was now a reality. Paul's conversion is not to be estimated by the exciting phenomena upon the Damascus Road. It is to be judged by its fruits. And what fruits followed! A new character, the far missionary journeys, the many churches founded, and the immortal letters!

Contrast Paul before and after his dramatic conversion. Who would dream that this rigid, Pharisaical Jew, breathing threatening and slaughter, making havoc of the church, bitter, narrow, cruel and sore in soul, a few years later would be writing, "Love suffereth long, and is kind; love envieth not; love vaunteth not itself, is not puffed up, doth not behave itself unseemly, seeketh not its own, is not provoked, . . . beareth all things, believeth all things, hopeth all things, endureth all things. Love never faileth."? Here is more than a changed man. *Here is another man.* Except for similarity of physical appearance and endowment of mind, *here is somebody else.* No longer a son of the Law, here is a *man in Christ.* Paul has become a new person in the Gospel. He became the authoritative example of his own words, "If any man is in Christ, he is a new creature," one of the "sons of light, and sons of the day."

The harsh young zealot has surrendered to The Way! This amazing news sped through the astonished church. Nothing comparable had occurred since Jesus' unexpected resurrection. Paul: convert! Christian! Thus the bravery of the little church conquered its arch enemy. The first Christians had won Paul, not by persuasive force of argument, but by sheer suffering. They had begun to win the world by out-suffering the world.

Chapter 3

THE EAGER APOSTLE

His Obscure Career

"Woe is unto me, if I preach not the gospel."

THE THIRD TIME we meet Paul, he is back in Damascus. "And straightway in the synagogues he proclaimed Jesus, that he is the Son of God." Immediately after his conversion, as we have seen, Paul had felt the missionary impulse. He began preaching to the Damascene Jews. So *The Acts* relates. And if we follow the story as it stands, and as it is generally interpreted, it continues as follows.

Paul's evangelizing career in Damascus was short. Quickly came the first attempt to take his life. His preaching excited the Damascene Jews to as hot a fury as he, himself, had known when he was imprisoning the disciples in Jerusalem. Fearing he might make his escape, his enemies "watched the gates also day and night that they might kill him." From Paul's own story in II *Corinthians*, we learn that they had the coöperation of the government officials. "In Damascus the governor under Aretas the King guarded the city of the Damascenes in order to take me: and through a window," aided by his disciples by night, "was I let down in a basket by the wall, and escaped his hand." Thus Paul, who once had planned to enter the city proudly and leave with much glory and human booty, now humiliatingly escaped in the dark, like a thief.

From Damascus, *The Acts* goes on, Paul went directly

to Jerusalem. There "he assayed to join himself to the disciples: and they were all afraid of him, not believing that he was a disciple." Why Paul returned directly to Jerusalem, we can only surmise. The church centered there. Its leaders were there. The believers whom he had persecuted and to whom he would wish to make amends were there. Also, his old associates whom he would desire to convert were there. Why those in the church "were all afraid of him" is plainer. Apparently they suspected that through the clever ruse of pretending to be a convert to The Way, he was hatching some more sinister plot against them. So they gave Paul an icy shoulder. "But Barnabas took him, and brought him to the apostles, and declared unto them how he had seen the Lord in the way, and that he had spoken to him, and how at Damascus he had preached boldly in the name of Jesus."

Immediately, according to *The Acts*, Paul began "preaching boldly in the name of the Lord: and he spake and disputed against the Grecian Jews." These were Greek-speaking Jews, like himself, and also like himself, immigrants into Jerusalem from gentile cities. He made no headway with them, for all the while "they were seeking to kill him." "When the brethren knew it" they realized that his only safety lay in flight. So to escape a second attack upon his life, "they brought him down to Caesarea, and sent him forth to Tarsus."

So Paul returned to his native city. Why did he go there? What did he do there? How long did he remain there? Neither *The Acts* nor his letters give us a knowledge of this period of his life.

Meanwhile the work in Syrian Antioch was flourishing. Evidently Barnabas, a Greek-speaking Jew from Cyprus, who had joined The Way, was a leader there. He needed some trained, zealous worker to assist him, and remembered

Paul. It may be that Paul, who never could be idle, had been successfully busy on a mission of his own in Tarsus and Cilicia, and his name was becoming known among Christians as an aggressive missionary. So Barnabas "went forth to Tarsus to seek for Saul; and when he had found him, he brought him unto Antioch." There in the teeming gentile city, Paul became a leader in the Christian fellowship. And there in Antioch one great day, as the church "ministered to the Lord, and fasted, the Holy Spirit said, Separate me Barnabas and Saul for the work whereunto I have called them." So entered Paul upon his immortal mission.

Thus runs the story of Paul according to *The Acts*. Its main points are clear. Paul, a persecutor of the Jerusalem Christians, was converted to The Way while on a mission to Damascus. Beginning to preach Christ in Damascus, he was compelled to flee for his life. Returning to Jerusalem, he was coldly received by the church until Barnabas guaranteed his sincerity. Again he was compelled to flee. He spent some time in his native Tarsus, whence Barnabas called him to assist in the work at Syrian Antioch. From thence Paul began his missionary journeys. So goes *The Acts* story.

Now we must pause. We come face to face with the most confusing problem in unravelling the data we possess on Paul's life. For in *Galatians*, Paul himself, taking an oath that "before God, I lie not," has an entirely different story to tell. "Then after three years [in Arabia and Damascus] I went up to Jerusalem to visit Cephas, and tarried with him fifteen days. But other of the apostles saw I none, save James the Lord's brother. . . . Then I came into the regions of Syria and Cilicia. And I was still unknown by face unto the churches of Judaea . . . but they only heard

28

say, He that once persecuted us now preacheth the faith.
. . . Then after the space of fourteen years I went up again
to Jerusalem with Barnabas." This is a very different picture from that given in *The Acts.* If it means what it says,
it declares that after Damascus Paul did no preaching in
Jerusalem. It states that his brief visit there was almost in
secret, and for the purpose as the Greek literally means, "to
become acquainted" with Peter. It affirms that not until
many years later did he again see Jerusalem. Even more
startlingly Paul says, "I was still unknown by face unto the
churches of Judaea . . . but they only heard say, He that
once persecuted us now preacheth the faith." If words mean
what they say, Paul's persecutions must have been carried
on *outside of Jerusalem and Judaea,* and not in them, as
The Acts declares, else he could not possibly have been "still
unknown by face unto the churches of Judaea." This means
that *The Acts* is mistaken as to the scene of Paul's persecuting activities. Also, it is probably in error about some
matters connected with his journeys, especially his activities
in Tarsus, Cilicia, and Syria, where he seems to have carried
on an effective work, perhaps even undertaking some considerable missionary journeying. Here are differences between
The Acts and the Epistles that can never be reconciled.[1]
What shall we make of them?

[1] This does not mean that everything in the two previous chapters is
null and void. Except for the exact locality of Paul's persecuting activities,
and his early preaching in Jerusalem, the picture is little changed. *The Acts*
apparently errs as to the *scene* of Paul's persecutions, but not that he was a
cruel persecutor. It seems to be mistaken about his first abortive preaching
in Jerusalem, but not in his evangelizing zeal for his brethren. It appears
to give too little significance to his first missionary endeavors in Cilicia, but
not to his work as a whole. It seems deliberately to have moved forward, as
we shall see, the date of the Jerusalem Council, but it is correct as to its
critical importance. While these and other like matters are of large import,
they do not belie the portrait as drawn. Criticism of details in *The Acts*
does not entail skepticism of it as a whole.

First, we must recognize the nature and purpose of *The Acts* and of Paul's letters. In neither is their primary intent that of giving material for a life of Paul. All references by Paul to himself in his letters are purely incidental to other more immediate concerns. He has no interest in his own biography. We cannot look to him for any organized data on his career.

Nor is it the intent of *The Acts* to give us the full story of Paul. Practically one half of the book deals with matters occurring before Paul enters the scene. The purpose of *The Acts* is larger than the career of Paul. Its business is to highlight the victorious spread of the Gospel. It is not finished history. Nor is it complete. It skips and jumps. It touches only the high points. Nor does it always place events in exact chronological order. In places it is at variance with statements Paul makes in his letters about himself. *The Acts* is plainly not intended to give us a biography of Paul, but rather the story of the Triumphant Gospel.

Take the engima of the Pauline chronology. *The Acts* and all Paul's letters yield us just three dates, and they are only approximate. When was Paul born? We do not know. How old was he when he was converted? Not a hint is given. How long after Pentecost did his Damascus Road experience occur? Not a figure can be detected. How long a period elapsed between his conversion and the start of his missionary campaigns? Except for the "three years" in Arabia and Damascus, all is a guess. How long did his missionary travels continue? Only loose estimates can be made. Just when did he die? The New Testament does not state. All our chronology of Paul must be made from three only approximate dates.

The first is given us by Paul himself. "In Damascus the governor under Aretas the King guarded the city of the

Damascenes in order to take me: and through a window was I let down in a basket by the wall, and escaped his hands." Now Damascus became, for a brief time, a part of Aretas' realm somewhere around 35 to 37 A.D. How long he had ruled when Paul fled Damascus we do not know. But it seems likely that these years fix rather closely the time of Paul's conversion.

The second date comes from *The Acts*. On his first visit to Corinth, Paul suffered another of those recurring riots which pursued his ministry. The storm broke "when Gallio was pro-consul of Achaia." From an ancient inscription we learn that Gallio's proconsulship was in 51–52 A.D. At this time Paul was in the midst of his Second Journey. From this date of 51–52, we can count back in *The Acts* to the approximate date when his missionary journeys began, though not with satisfactory exactness.

The third date, again from *The Acts*, concerns Paul's final arrest in Jerusalem. When Paul was seized in the Holy City, Felix was the Roman governor in Palestine. "But when two years were fulfilled Felix was succeeded by Porcius Festus." Festus we know came to power about 55–57. So Paul, being arrested two years previously, was imprisoned around 53–55.

Paul, himself, gives us a fourth figure. It is not a date, but a stretch of time. It is the famous "fourteen years." After describing his conversion, and his stay in Tarsus when he "came into the regions of Syria and Cilicia," he adds, "Then after the space of fourteen years I went up again to Jerusalem." This "again" seems to mean that this visit occurred fourteen years "after [the] three years [when] I went up to Jerusalem to visit Cephas, and tarried with him fifteen days," though we cannot be fully sure. It may mean fourteen years after his conversion near Damascus.

31

In II *Corinthians* Paul again refers to a vision and to a period of fourteen years. "I know a man in Christ, fourteen years ago . . . such a one caught up even to the third heaven." The question inevitably arises: do these two accounts refer to the same vision and the same fourteen years? That a man should have two visions, each of them fitting neatly into a fourteen-year period of reckoning is most surprising. These accounts *may* refer to different visions, though it is more likely Paul is speaking of the *same* spiritual event. But we cannot be sure. Since we do not know the precise dating of II *Corinthians*, as Paul dated none of his letters, we cannot be certain just when this fourteen-year period opened and closed.

Thus no exact chronology of Paul's life can ever be figured out. The necessary data do not exist. Much of his career must remain forever obscure.

What is the ordinary reader to do? He can, if he chooses, side with *The Acts* against Paul in his own letters. He can close his eyes to all differences between Paul's own statements and those in *The Acts*. But surely this is folly. For it is indisputable that Paul's own statements about himself are to be accepted before every other witness.

Or, second, he may, if he chooses, stick to Paul's letters alone, largely ignoring *The Acts*. This many scholars do. But there is too much plainly authentic material in *The Acts*, even though it does not always fit neatly together, or even match with Paul's own statements, for *The Acts* to be so largely set aside.

In the third place, the student may take a compromising, harmonizing attitude. He may try as far as possible to dovetail together the material in *The Acts* with that given in the letters. That is, with marked limitations, the method of this book. But this also has its dangers. It frankly is a compromise, and as such can never be wholly satisfactory. There are contradictions that can never be reconciled. Gaps exist that can never be filled. And in harmonization, too much is apt to depend upon guesses and surmises. The final result must be fragmentary, and full of uncertainties. But, if cautiously used, it is the best method we possess at present for working out any reasonably effective knowledge of the Great Apostle.[2]

All this should not alarm the reader. When one realizes that the biographical material in Paul's letters is but incidental, and that the Pauline career in *The Acts* is but an outline, used by the author not to magnify Paul, but to glorify the spread of the Gospel, these many discrepancies will cease to trouble him.

Despite these uncertainties, what authoritative picture of Paul do we finally possess? In briefest summary it is this: Paul, a Jew of Tarsus, a man full of zeal and energy, upon meeting some of the first Christians, embarked upon a furious career of cruel persecution, laying waste the church and seeking its extermination. In the midst of these terrors he received in a vision a revelation of the Risen Jesus which revolutionized his character. After an uncertain period spent in Arabia, Syria, and Cilicia, during which he may have undertaken some of his large evangelizing efforts, he was called to Syrian Antioch, from whence he continued his ever-enlarging missionary career.

Here lives the Hellenistic Jew, the Roman citizen, the fervent fanatic, the cruel persecutor, the glad convert, the eager disciple, and the burning missionary. He who counted himself "the least of the apostles . . . because I persecuted

[2] For a brief, non-technical exposition of the general trustworthiness of *The Acts* see *One Lord, One Faith*, by Floyd V. Filson, Chap. 2, Westminster Press, Philadelphia, 1943.

the church," had become the zealous apostle, so ardent that in the years to come he could with sincerity write, "For I reckon that I am not a whit behind the very chiefest apostles" because "I labored more abundantly than they all: yet not I, but the grace of God which was with me." "Woe is unto me, if I preach not the gospel."

Chapter 4

THE PIONEER MISSIONARY

THE PRINCIPLES AND METHODS OF HIS CAMPAIGNS

"The love of Christ constraineth us."

THE WORLD SITUATION in Paul's day favored missionary effort.[1] Never an easy enterprise, missionary endeavor has always had to fight its way. But some periods of human history have been more open to religious propaganda than others. Paul's time was most friendly to wandering champions of religious faiths. The whole situation conspired to make the proclamation of the Gospel warmly welcome.

There was a world government. All that the first Christians knew as civilization was enclosed in the far-reaching union of the Roman Empire. Roman authority meted out justice from the borders of Scotland to the gates of India. Roman governors kept law and order from desert fringes to forest borders. Rome's soldiers, policing the Empire, suppressed piracy and brigandage, and maintained peace.

Within this vast iron military unity a wide latitude of local freedom was permitted. Under Rome-appointed governors backed by imperial soldiers, the variegated provinces

[1] This book, not being a commentary on *The Acts*, makes no attempt to follow Paul's journeys point by point. Tracing his journeys is sixth-grade geography. The reader should skim through *The Acts* 13–28, tracing out Paul's routes with the aid of maps provided on the end papers of this volume. What is given here are the principles, motives and methods underlying Paul's journeys, showing why, not just where Paul traveled.

were permitted to keep their local customs, laws and religious beliefs. So long as they paid taxes, sent the stipulated tribute to Rome, and dwelt in peace, they were largely unmolested. In many of its aspects the benevolent Empire offered more adequate life than had the continuous hostilities of independent petty principalities. Except for the presence of the Roman governor, the Roman constabulary and the tribute tax, life went on much as before. Because of the easier, safer travel and the enforced peace, it was both freer and more prosperous.

On occasion, as we have seen, Rome granted special boons to favored citizens, certain provinces were made Roman colonies, and certain cities made Roman communities. Such colonies and cities were freed from various restrictions. However, they were required upon all occasions to keep the peace. Riot or revolt meant the swift revocation of these special rights. At the time of the great riot in the theater at Ephesus, it was the possible loss of these privileges that haunted the town clerk, and finally stilled the mob. His quiet admonition was enough, "For indeed we are in danger to be accused concerning this day's riot, there being no cause for it: and as touching it we shall not be able to give account of this concourse." Of course the Ephesians slipped home in silence!

World government meant also world peace. The Roman peace was probably the most famous peace in human history. Not before, and rarely if ever since, has a period of general peace been so widespread or so long enduring. To be sure, it was the enforced peace of empire, won and maintained at the sword's point, but it was a peace that smothered the petty hostilities of the world's minor nations. This universal peace made possible a richer life and allowed a freedom of movement impossible in war, or even forbiden between hostile peoples. Anyone within the Empire could travel freely any time, to any place. He was always under the one government, one law, and one protection. Whatever his business, he was free to promote it as widely as he would. Hence we find Paul moving freely through Syria, Cilicia, Cyprus, Pamphilia, Galatia, Asia, Macedonia, and Achaia, and planning visits to Rome, southern Gaul and distant Spain. Under the Roman peace all the Empire lay opened wide.

World peace meant world travel. The central Mediterranean Sea, which Rome had cleared of pirates, was an open highway to everywhere of importance. The great cities of Alexandria, Caesarea, Tyre, Sidon, Antioch, Tarsus, Ephesus, Troas, Thessalonica and Corinth, which ringed the eastern Mediterranean and Aegean, were in direct sailing connection with each other and Rome. The importance of the Mediterranean as an open highway becomes doubly clear when we note that in Paul's years of travels and miles of journeys, about half the total distance he covered was across the waters of this azure inland sea.

Besides this natural highway for ships, the famous Roman roads linked the Empire together. In Paul's part of the Roman world various interconnecting routes ran across Thrace, Macedonia, Asia Minor and along the Syrian coast. These post roads were well built, well maintained, well guarded, and well traveled. They insured safe, speedy travel for the interchange of goods, peoples, and above all ideas. Men traveled for pleasure, for governmental affairs, military missions, business enterprise and the spreading of various beliefs and faiths. The book of *Revelation*, written a generation after Paul's day, gives a vivid glimpse of the world trade that flowed across the Empire toward Rome. "Gold, and silver, and precious stones, and pearls, and fine linen,

and purple, and silk, and scarlet; and all thyine wood, and
. . . ivory, and . . . most precious wood, and . . . brass, and
iron, and marble; and cinnamon, and spice, and incense
and ointment, and frankincense, and wine, and oil, and
fine flour, and wheat, and cattle, and sheep; and merchan-
dise of horses and chariots and slaves; and souls of men."
It was over these highways, teeming with staples, luxuries
armaments and human beings, that Paul hurried, offering
in city after city his most valuable of all goods, the
Gospel.

Moreover, a world language facilitated world travel and
trade. Except in the small back-country towns, like Lystra
Greek was everywhere readily understood. And even there
as the story of Paul's mission indicates, many had a sufficient smattering of Greek to make themselves understood
Greek thought, Greek speech, and Greek culture were
everywhere. Although local dialects flourished, all Paul's
preaching seems to have been done in Greek, and all his
letters certainly are in Greek. This universality of Greek
greatly speeded the spread of the Good News. The ham-
pering restrictions that modern languages put upon today's
missionary efforts were unknown to Paul. No tedious
years needed to be spent in the slow, difficult mastery
of a strange vocabulary, grammar and pronunciation. No
precious time was lost because a missionary, after painfully
arriving at a partial mastery of one new tongue, was still
debarred from another district, speaking a yet stranger language. Any Christian like Paul, with a propagandizing impulse, could begin at once, go immediately anywhere, and
move from place to place as rapidly and as often as necessity required. Moreover, each province, whatever its dialect,
could hear the Gospel in a familiar tongue. For though
Greek might not be the everyday speech of the locality,

many natives would be passably familiar with it. They were not compelled to hear the Good News in mispronounced words and butchered grammar, with a strong foreign accent, from the lisping lips of a missionary who, by force of birth, could never more than partially master their language. Indeed, the probabilities are that when they first heard the Gospel from Paul's lips they heard it in a more correct and more effective Greek than they, themselves, could command. Much of Paul's speedy success is due in part to this universality of the Greek tongue.

A world-wide religious restlessness was another general feature of Paul's Roman world. The decay of belief in the Greek and Roman pantheons left a religious void. Men who could no longer believe in Zeus, Jupiter, Athena, Venus and all the childish legends of the gods had nothing to fill their hunger for a faith. They were seeking news of gods in whom sensible and sincere men could trust. Philosophies like Epicureanism or Stoicism might satisfy the pleasure-loving, the puritan-minded, or the stout-hearted. For the mass of men they brought no sufficient message of salvation. Barbarian cruelties, universal vice, absurd idolatries, benumbing superstitions, terrifying demonologies, and brutal slavery made daily life a torment. For these ills the old, the stated religions offered no relief. The Roman world lay ready for any message presenting itself as good news with hope and power.

This wide religious ferment was being met in Paul's day in two ways. First: by what the scholars now call the "Mystery Religions." The restless gentiles in their religious hunger were adopting renovated religions from the ancient east, spread abroad by wandering religious teachers. These Mystery Religions were of a rich variety, the best of them offering three elements for which the human heart deeply longs. By a series of private initiation rites, which partly accounts for their being called "mystery," the seeker wa introduced into the particular religion of his choice. By these secret acts he believed he entered into direct and complete fellowship with his god. He knew his god and was in union with him. Thus he received what was to him salvation. Henceforth his life was in the safekeeping of his god He was thus assured of immortality, physical death having no power to separate him from his deity. In some cases his initiation rites included a dramatic pageant of the life, and sometimes of the death and rising, of his god. Thus, as it were, he saw his god face to face. In a general way, because, like "evolution" and "relativity" with us, the jargon of these Mystery Religions was in the air, all this was familiar to Paul. Many phrases in his letters echo the words and ideas these religions used to win converts from their unhappy religious void to nobler faith.

The other means by which this religious restlessness was being answered was by the Jewish Diaspora, or Dispersion. For several centuries the Jews had been scattered throughout the great cities and larger towns of the Empire. With them they had taken their Mosaic faith and synagogue services. Every Roman city with a sufficient Jewish population had one or more synagogues. There from Sabbath to Sabbath the children of Abraham met for worship. The building was a plain meeting house. The service was simple and austere. There was no image, no altar, no priest, no sacrifice. The sacred scriptures were read, prayers said, psalms sung, and the Law expounded. Undergirding all was the belief in God, a spirit, one and invisible, whom no image could depict, and who dwelt with his people, and demanded of them righteousness. This simple, clean worship awed many a gentile, who could not endure the ornate rituals, the gross superstitions and low morals of his native religion. Having thrown away his idols, he was irresistibly drawn to the Jewish synagogue services. Some were so moved that they eventually adopted the Jewish faith as their own. They became proselytes, were circumcised, accepted the Jewish dietary rules, and became to all practical purposes in the matter of religion, Jews, true sons of Abraham. Others did not go so far. They could not accept circumcision and the food restrictions. But they remained friendly adherents. They accepted the great moral implications of the scriptures and believed in the one true God. Still classed as gentiles, they were morally and religiously good Jews.

For Paul, both these initiates into the Mystery Religions and the gentiles accepted into the Jewish faith, or who were in open sympathy with it, proved fertile ground for the Gospel seed. Their religious earnestness made them ready heeders of yet better Good News. Already the latter were believers in the great bases of his own faith.

Finally, there was a world-wide religious freedom. In Paul's time Rome allowed full liberty of worship. Her insistence upon Emperor worship did not begin until a generation later. The Empire was used to wandering religious teachers proclaiming new faiths. In the eyes of the public, Paul, as journeying religionist, would seem neither strange nor queer. He was just another peripatetic teacher who thought he had found the true light, and was going about seeking to enlighten the world. The curious, the careless and the earnest would stop to hear him. It might be that he had something to offer.

Here, then, was Paul's world as he began his herculean journeys. All its basic conditions favored him: a world government, world peace, world travel, world language, world

41

restlessness, and world religious freedom. So much that today hampers and complicates missionary enterprise was then non-existent. There was no need to secure passports, learn new languages, build churches, chapels, schools, hospitals, asylums and compounds. The work could begin in synagogues, and when they were lacking or closed or inconvenient, homes, hired halls, market places and street corners sufficed. Therefore, expenses were small. Missionaries could travel on their own, earn their way, and when taken in, dwell with their converts. All of which things Paul did. By the grace of a blessed providence, when Paul was ready, the world was ready.

All this did not mean freedom from obstacles. Paul's missionary labors were hampered by gruelling hardships, and hindered by harsh difficulties. In the matter of distance alone, just the effort to get over the ground must have been exhausting. Even today, with the conveniences of luxury liners, Pullman cars, rubber-cushioned busses, planned and conducted tours, and good hotels, travel is tiring. In those days of journeys afoot, by donkey and camelback, the traveler had to make his own way, sleeping in bug-ridden khans, eating unwholesome food, and always exposed to the open weather of blazing sun, chilling winds, drenching rains and freezing snows. Voyaging by boat was no better. Crowded together, eating indifferent food, tossed by the waves and seasick, soaked by the stinging salt spume and battered by storms, the voyagers prayed for land. Certainly Paul never traveled for pleasure!

It is impossible to total the mileage of Paul's journeys exactly. A careful estimate, based on *The Acts*, which can never be more than rough approximation, gives the round sum of ten thousand miles. Of these ten thousand miles,

bout half were overland, and half by sea. As between sea
nd land, the discomforts of one equalled the burdens of
he other. While these ten thousand miles are hardly a
tarter as compared with Wesley's five thousand miles a
ear for nearly half a century, they were a hundred times
nore trying. Nor do they equal the danger, enervation and
listance of Livingstone's explorations, but they were just as
aeroic. Fortunately, however obscure may be the mileage,
peed of travel, and exact routes of Paul's journeys, we are
aot left in the dark concerning his hardships.

There were the perils of land travel: "In journeyings
often, in perils of rivers, in perils of robbers, . . . in perils in
the city, in perils in the wilderness, . . . in watchings often,
in hunger and thirst, in fastings often, in cold and nakedness." In spite of the well-guarded Roman roads, travel had
its incessant dangers. Guerrillas in swift raids would sweep
down upon some lonely band of travelers, strip them
of valuables, and make a speedy getaway. On byroads, the
dangers were worse, more frequent, and progress slower.
The chilled waters of bridgeless rivers had to be forded. If
one could not make the next town or khan, one might have
to spend a sleepless, supperless night out in the cold. If
robbed—and Paul hints he suffered from many holdups—
one had to trudge minus one's donkey, with clothes and
money gone, cold and hungry, until one met a friendly
passer-by, or arrived at the next haven.

In the city lurked footpads, rabble rousers, brutal police
and stormy rioters. Nearly every city's name recalled a riot
to Paul: Pisidian Antioch, Iconium, Lystra, Philippi, Thessalonica, Corinth, Ephesus, and Jerusalem. Riotous cities
all. In his letters Paul had no occasion to recall the many
sunny days, the austere mountain scenery and the over-
powering glory of Levantine beauty. What he had double

43

reason to remember was the cold, hunger, sleeplessness, and hairbreadth escapes.

The perils of ocean voyaging were as great. "In perils in the sea," "thrice I suffered shipwreck, a night and a day have I been in the deep." Where and when these three shipwrecks occurred is unrecorded in *The Acts*. One of them, Paul remembered, left him swimming in the sea for "a night and a day." From twelve to twenty-four hours, probably clinging to some broken spar, he struggled in the raging main until, battered and half-drowned, he was washed, cold and exhausted, upon a beach. To these three shipwrecks must be added a fourth on his voyage to Rome. For Paul's record of the three wrecks was made before that last long sailing. As described at length in *The Acts*, it must have been one of the great sea storms of history. A howling winter northeaster roared in unrelieved fury for the unbelievable duration of two full weeks. No glimpse of sun or star by which sailors then steered was possible, and the boat was to all practical purposes lost in the boiling waste. The story ends vividly with the ship beached on a bar, thrashed by thunderous rollers, and the passengers washed through the breakers, getting ashore in the cold rain of chilly dawn. Paul could hardly have taken ship for pleasure.

The perils from his enemies were worse than those of nature. They were more relentless, and pointed with cunning. "In prisons more abundantly, in stripes above measure, in deaths oft." Exactly how many times Paul was jailed we have no record. Philippi, Jerusalem, Caesarea and Rome, that is the account. But the latter three came after this statement, "In prisons more abundantly." He must have had others not now known. But where, and how many times? At Ephesus almost surely, but the rest cannot be guessed. For the most part in the usual oriental prisons,

44

horrible holes, often underground dungeons, without ventilation or sanitation, and crawling with vermin. Darkness, stench, lice, stocks and irons ruled, until some kinder justice rescued.

"Of the Jews five times received I forty stripes save one." Only one of these, at Philippi, is recorded in *The Acts*. These were terrible lashings that ripped open the back. How Paul must have agonized at the prospect of a second, a third, a fourth, and a fifth. As if these were not enough, 'thrice was I beaten with rods." None of these *The Acts* mentions, but Paul could never forget them. To the five lashings were added the three beatings. Eight times his back was stripped and beaten to blood. One wonders, how did he ever survive? "Once was I stoned." That, according to *The Acts*, was at Lystra. It was no make-believe affair. The mob threw to kill, and killed they thought they had, leaving Paul lying outside the city as one dead. But a few friends, on going out to secure his body, perceived a spark of life. They carried him into the city, and the next day got him, all black and blue, away to safety. "In perils from the Gentiles" who trumped up charges, as at Philippi and Ephesus, accusing him of sedition. Their real reason, however, was the fear that if Paul's mission succeeded, their questionable incomes would cease. So came riots and arrests, beatings and stocks in city after city. Paul never preached for his health!

The perils from his fellow Jews were perhaps the most painful of all Paul's bitter experiences. "In perils from mine countrymen . . . in perils among false brethren." Jews in gentile lands should have been kindly to a brother Jew, a stranger in a strange land, whose only offense was a new interpretation of the old Law. They might not agree with him, but nothing he said justified their malice and brutality.

45

Continually they battered him, rioting in Pisidian Antioch, Iconium, Lystra, Corinth and Jerusalem. As for the "false brethren," they were fellow Jewish followers of the Lord who when they turned Christian, could not let go the intricacies of the Mosaic law. They demanded that every gentile convert keep the whole law to its last detail. When Paul refused to require circumcision and food restriction from his gentile converts, these brethren hounded his trail, disrupted his churches, pursued him to Jerusalem for a show down, demanding that he be silenced. How hot their malice was, and how ardent their endeavors, Paul's vehement rejoinder in *Galatians* testifies. Paul had to carry on, not with the acquiescence of his fellow Jews, and the aid of his fellow Jewish Christians, but in the face of their malicious hatred and strenuous obstruction.

Finally, to all this suffering was added the burden of "anxiety for all the churches." As if scourgings, beatings, stoning, shipwrecks, mobs, robbings, imprisonments, cold, hunger, illness, sleeplessness, and persecutions from fellow Jews, besides the support of himself and his fellow workers, and his incessant preaching of the Gospel and founding of churches were not enough! In addition to these "labors more abundantly" wherein he "labored more abundantly than they all," there was the necessity of revisiting, usually at great risk, church after church, to warn, instruct and encourage. In addition, letter after letter had to be composed, dictated and despatched. "Besides those things that are without, there is that which presseth upon me daily, anxiety for all the churches."

We would call it enough had Paul just traveled easily with his expenses paid, preached his Gospel, won his converts, written his letters and organized his churches. These would have been a remarkable achievement, equalled by few in Christian history. But these, his main tasks, seem beside his suffering as almost a side issue. What pain, what fortitude, what endurance and what scars lie back of his words, "I bear branded on my body the marks of Jesus."

But such a fragmentary description fails to make vividly poignant the story of Paul's agonies. The passage just given in broken fragments should be read whole for what it is, a great prose poem, stung from Paul by harsh critics who should have been his eager supporters; a poem which depicts his unflinching sufferings for Christ.

> In labors more abundantly,
> In prisons more abundantly,
> In stripes above measure,
>> In deaths oft.
>
> Of the Jews
> Five times received I forty stripes save one.
>
> Thrice was I beaten with rods,
> Once was I stoned,
> Thrice I suffered shipwreck,
> A night and a day have I been in the deep;
>
> In journeyings often,
> In perils of rivers,
> In perils of robbers,
> In perils from my countrymen,
> In perils from the Gentiles,
> In perils in the city,
> In perils in the wilderness,
> In perils in the sea;
> In perils among false brethren;
>
> In labor and travail,
> In watchings often,
> In hunger and thirst,
> In fastings often,
>> In cold and nakedness.

> Beside those things that are without,
> There is that which presseth upon me daily,
> Anxiety for all the churches.

What induced Paul to endure such sufferings? What compelled him year after year to face repeated scourgings and imprisonments? What all-consuming motive forced him on? He, himself, tells us in one short glorious phrase "The love of Christ constraineth us." This might mean only, 'Christ hems me in.' But more probably it means either, 'Christ's love within me drives me on,' or 'The love I bear for Christ compels me.' Most probably Paul means both. For of all factors in Paul's life, none is more certain than the moving love of Christ within him, and his own radiant love that flamed in gratitude for all that Christ had done for him. "I have been crucified with Christ; and it is no longer I that live, but Christ liveth in me: and that life which I now live in the flesh I live in faith, the faith which is in the Son of God, who loved me, and gave himself up for me." "I am debtor both to Greeks and to Barbarians both to the wise and to the foolish." I am debtor not merely for what they have contributed to me, but for what I have received from Christ which they so sorely need. I owe it to them to share with them this redeeming love of Christ Preach I must. "For woe is unto me, if I preach not the gospel." Keep silent I cannot, whatever the persecutions Each is "the brother for whose sake Christ died." "The love of Christ constraineth us."

But a constraining motive, however noble, is not enough To succeed one needs also an effective plan. Paul had such a plan. Whether he worked it out before he began his journeys, developed it as he went along, and whether it owed much to the suggestions of others, we cannot know

48

Probably all three were contributing factors. But a survey of Paul's work shows a clear plan that has in it the insight of an organizing genius.

All Paul's methods centered about one vivid aim: *To capture the whole Roman Empire for Christ.* At heart Paul was a spiritual imperialist. Nothing less than the mighty world government, with all its various peoples, would satisfy the ambitions of his heart. The whole wide world for Christ! "Till we all attain unto the unity of the faith," and "Christ is all, and in all." His great problem was, how can the Empire with its peoples be won to the Lord Christ most quickly, easily and permanently. To this end, instinctively or from deliberate study, Paul followed a basic plan.

First, he sought to establish a *chain of Christian communities* in the great metropolitan centers across the Empire, from Jerusalem to Rome, and beyond. If he could win the cities, he could win the Empire. Already churches flourished in the coastal cities up the Syrian seaboard, from Jerusalem to Antioch. Now let them be extended into every key city across the Empire! To win the cities would be to lay the Empire at the feet of Christ.

To this end Paul visited only new territory. He would not build on others' foundations. That would waste time. Also, it might create jealousies. So Paul pioneered. His pioneering was thus a matter of conviction, but it was partly the irresistible expression of an inborn aptitude. Paul was by nature a pioneer. His restless spirit had to be on the move. "It was the good pleasure of God, who separated me even from my mother's womb, and called me through his grace, to reveal his Son in me, that I might preach him among the Gentiles." It was his divine assignment to invade new territory, win the gentiles, and take the Empire for his Lord.

He stopped, therefore, only in the great urban centers.

49

27016

The smaller towns and villages he by-passed. The great cities, he knew, would become evangelizing centers for the surrounding territory. People coming into the city would pick up the Gospel story and carry it home. Christian converts in the city would take the Good News to the neighboring towns. Pisidian Antioch would become the evangelizing center for Galatia, Philippi for Macedonia, Corinth for Achaia, and Ephesus for Asia. It is quite probable that Paul stopped only in the great cities, partly because he was himself urban born, trained and minded. But he could, if occasion demanded, work effectively in smaller communities like Iconium, Lystra and Derbe. Though Paul's natural bent for city life is important, it is secondary. Paul saw that the cities were the key to the Empire. Win them and win all.

Even in the great cities Paul was content with small beginnings. A synagogue with a handful of Jews in Pisidian Antioch, a street corner crowd in Lystra, a few women by the riverbank in Philippi, a married couple, Aquila and Priscilla, in teeming Corinth. Appearing unknown and unheralded, Paul began among the lowly and the obscure wherever the smallest opportunity offered. Often his temple was a smoky kitchen, his rostrum a street curb, his congregation humble manual laborers of the marketplace. Imperial as were his ambitions for Christ, Paul despised not "the day of small things." Wherever two or three were gathered together, there was Paul eager to start.

If possible, most naturally he first visited the Jewish synagogue. Doubtless he did this in part from patriotic loyalty. He was a Jew, and desired to be with his fellow Jews. As a Jew he longed to bring his compatriots to Christ. But he had a deeper reason for beginning in the·synagogues. The people frequenting them offered the most promising field for immediate results. There the one true God was known and worshipped. There the scriptures were read and believed. There the promise of the expected One gave immediate contact with the story of Jesus. There worshipped devout gentile proselytes and sympathizers, already freed from their polytheism and idolatry. No arguments were needed to convince them concerning monotheism and the one true God. They needed only winning to the yet more excellent way. Here in the synagogue the field was already ripe for harvest.

When preaching Christ in the synagogue failed, Paul turned directly to the gentiles. He wasted no time on hopeless situations. Once the synagogue slammed its doors in his face, he permitted himself no useless, mournful regrets. His gospel was to all men, "to the Jew first, and also to the Greek."

Always Paul supported himself. He was at pains "that, when I preach the gospel, I may make the gospel without charge." Though he believed "that they that proclaim the gospel should live of the gospel," he earned his way. His reason was to prevent the insinuation, 'He's in it for the money.' The Empire was full of wandering religious teachers like himself, many of whom were mountebanks. They grabbed what gain they could, or if possible settled down to live off their converts. Paul sought to avoid the slightest appearance of such practices. Moreover his preaching stirred up persecutions. Soon he would have to flee. If he took money and then fled, his enemies could make big capital out of it. 'See what fools you are,' they could say to his converts. 'That little money-hungry preacher came here with his silly gospel, and like fools you believed him. He passed the hat and like easy marks you contributed. When the storm broke, as he knew it would, he cleared out, money and all, leaving you holding the bag, to face the music alone.

Clever rascal, he.' So Paul foreswore his right to be supported by the Gospel that he might "cause no hindrance to the gospel of Christ." Only after a church was established would he receive a contribution for his welfare. Even then the church initiated the offering. It was their voluntary gift. However great might be his need, he never requested money for himself. But it is good to report that in his distress, his churches, especially Philippi several times, sent him funds to relieve his wants. Beyond such gifts he took nothing for himself. He would rather suffer pecuniary lack that his Gospel might be kept above the suspicion of sordid gain.

Having founded his churches, Paul went to great labor to keep in touch with them. He was no coward fleeing at the first flurry of danger, never to be seen again. He was no irresponsible evangelist who invaded a town with a flourish, in excitement won his converts, and then rushed off, leaving them to swim or perish. Paul built to last. He revisited his friends, advised, wrote to, and organized them, because above all he loved them.

According to the New Testament record, which is by no means complete, Paul visited Pisidian Antioch, Iconium, Lystra, Derbe and Corinth at least four times each. He stopped in Philippi and Thessalonica three times. He was in Ephesus twice, and had an additional special meeting for counsel and farewells with the Ephesian elders at nearby Miletus. In addition, *The Acts* account indicates that he was so well known in Berea, Troas, and Assos, that these and probably other like places must have seen his face many times. How frequently he returned to encourage and counsel his converts can be realized when we find his visits to his eight chief churches totalled no less than twenty-nine. He was bent on seeing his work thoroughly stabilized, and growing. He trained young men like Silas, Timothy and

Titus as assistants, that they might strengthen the work, and carry on in his stead. He built for permanency.

Finally, he tied his churches together. He originated a kind of connectional system. The importance of this effort cannot be over-estimated. We think of Christianity as composed of millions of adherents scattered the world over, with churches by the thousand on as many prominent street corners. But it was not so in Paul's day. There was not a church building anywhere in the whole vast Empire. Christians numbered but tiny handfuls. They were mostly lowly, persecuted folk from the cities' poorer quarters. They were isolated, weak and endangered. They needed a consciousness of their bigness, strength and unity. To this end Paul tried to bind his churches together in a unity of fellowship, a bond of brotherhood. They could help each other in need, gain a vision of the sweep of the Christian movement, realize that they possessed an unquenchable power, and see that together their increasing numbers made toward a mighty, conquering host. This unity Paul hoped would become the unifying center of a divided world. He saw that human unity would never come by force of Empire. Only Christian love could unify divided humanity. Only in Christ could humanity "put on the new man . . . after the image of him that created him: where there cannot be Greek and Jew, circumcision and uncircumcision, barbarian, Scythian, bondman, freeman." To that end he risked his life. For his promoting the unity of his gentile churches with the mother church at Jerusalem became the immediate cause of his final arrest and martyrdom. But at whatever cost to himself, his churches must know themselves as one, and as the world's unifying center. In them was "one faith, one baptism" which would reunite "all things in Christ" who "is all, and in all."

This was the amazing strategy of Paul. How far he fore-planned it, how much he worked it out as he went along, how greatly others advised him, and how richly it was given him in the Spirit, is of little moment now. Probably all were contributing factors. Starting as an unknown evangelist, invading new territory, going directly to the great urban centers, stopping first at Jewish synagogues, beginning in small ways with pick-up groups, supporting himself, revisiting, writing to and strengthening his little churches, suffering indescribable ignominies and cruelties, this pioneer missionary, moved by the constraining love of Christ, foresaw and worked toward the eventual unity of divided humanity under the transforming grace of Christ, who is all and in all, blessed forever.

Chapter 5

THE PASTOR LETTER-WRITER

His Letters: Their Writing

"Anxiety for all the churches"

PAUL'S EPISTLES are *letters*. Except for *Romans*, they are neither books nor treatises. A treatise presents its subject upon, say, "The Sailing of Catboats," or "The Chemical History of Nylon," in systematic order. It carefully organizes such facts, arguments and explanations as are necessary to clarify the subject. But letters are free, spontaneous, casual writings, with little logical sequence. Except, then, for *Romans*, which is a short treatise on Paul's Gospel, all his epistles are letters, and must be read as letters.

In all ages letters have possessed certain common characteristics. They are relatively brief. There are long letters, and some of Paul's letters like I *Corinthians*, which by modern standards would run to some thirty-five pages, are long. But as compared with even short books, letters are brief. Letters also are informal. Their style is familiar, even intimate, skipping from topic to topic without exact outline, full of interruptions, and grammatical slips and ambiguities. They are personal and semi-private. Rarely intended to be preserved or made generally public, they contain references to mutual knowledge never fully understood by outsiders.

These facts must be remembered as one reads Paul's letters. They account for the lack of logical outlines, the sudden interruptions in thought, loose style, broken sentences, sudden asides, omission of details, and obscure personal references which, while quite inappropriate in public documents, are characteristic of all private correspondence.

Paul's *method* of writing was by dictation. Dictation usually results in an easy informality. It is seldom so succinct and orderly as writing. Unless it is thoroughly corrected and rewritten, it will remain relatively rough and wordy. Except for *Romans*, which Paul seems to have worked over in his mind for a long while, and certain other sections of his letters like the *Love* and *Immortality* chapters in I *Corinthians* 13 and 15, which have the high polish of careful poetry, Paul's letters bear all the marks of rapid dictation. Apparently when he had thought out in a general way what he wished to say, Paul called for writing materials and an amanuensis, and hurriedly began dictating. He signed off with his own hand, and being a busy man, let it go at that. The manuscript was not, in his mind, inspired scripture, but only a personal letter of little lasting importance, and concerned only with an immediate, temporary problem. Correction and polish were unessential.

That Paul dictated his letters is clear just from reading them. But by indirection he says he dictated. At the letter's close, he customarily took the pen from his amanuensis and added something in his own bold hand. "See," he says toward the end of *Galatians*, "with how large letters I write unto you with mine own hand." In II *Thessalonians* he is more emphatic, introducing the closing benediction with, "The salutation of me Paul with mine own hand, which is the token in every epistle: so I write." In *Romans* Paul's 'stenographer' himself interrupts with, "I Tertius, who write the epistle [at Paul's dictation], salute you."

The rushing, staccato beat in the letters' phrases suggests that Paul, quick, eager, hurried, often excited, and in the case of *Galatians* angered, dictated as he paced the room. One can almost hear the quick tramp of his feet march in his sentences. One must, therefore, look upon these epistles *first* as occasional letters, tossed off in the busy heat of a hurried life, by a hard-pressed man to hard-pressed friends.

The *form* of Paul's letters followed the conventional plan of his day. Today our method is: the place, date, addressee, 'Dear So and So'; then the letter itself, and finally the writer's 'Yours truly, So and So.' The plan has advantages. We know at once whence the letter comes, when it was written, and we reach the contents immediately. Its disadvantage is that, upon receiving a letter, one must glance first at the letter's end to discover the writer. Yet we must know the writer first if we are to understand the letter. In Paul's day, the writer's name came first, and was followed immediately by the addressee's name. "Irene to Taomorphris and Philo good comfort," began an ancient letter. So Paul opens his letters: "Paul, a servant of Jesus Christ . . . to all that are in Rome." "Paul, called to be an apostle of Jesus Christ . . . unto the church of God which is at Corinth." The place of writing and date of dictating, Paul, following the general custom of his day, omits entirely. His readers knew.

Once having begun a letter, Paul regularly followed a general outline:

The Salutation: Paul, to the church at ——
Thanksgiving and Prayer: I thank God always ——
Doctrinal Discussion of the Subject in Hand: For I would have you know ——

Practical Application of the Principles Discussed: Walk worthily ——

Personal Greetings: The brethren that are with me salute you ——

Benediction: The grace of the Lord Jesus Christ be with your Spirit.

Except for *Galatians*, which omits the Thanksgiving, this is Paul's standardized plan. But within this stereotyped outline Paul followed no rigid order. Dictated, loosely constructed and full of asides, the Doctrinal and Practical sections do not proceed in a straight line. Topics begun are interrupted, and sometimes left unfinished. Because the letters were private and for an immediate purpose they do not, even when all taken together, afford total data for a full summary of Paul's rich thought. One does not so completely unload one's self in casual letters.

The *number* of Paul's authentic letters is in dispute. The reader of the King James Version of the New Testament will find fourteen letters ascribed to Paul. Of these it is sure that *Hebrews* was *not* written by Paul. It has no salutation, "Paul, an apostle of Jesus Christ." It does not, after Paul's invariable custom, salute some particular church. It does not follow Paul's regular outline. Its highly polished Greek and smooth sentences are not in Paul's blunt style. Its great description of Faith in chapter eleven is different in conception and meaning from Paul's own declaration of Salvation by Faith. As far back as that great church father, Origen (about A.D. 185–254), and through the long centuries since, no informed person has believed that Paul wrote *Hebrews*. The caption in the King James Version, "The Epistle of Paul to the Hebrews," is not part of the original manuscript. It is a late and mistaken editorial addition ascribing the letter to Paul. All other New Testament letters have some great name connected with them. But *Hebrews* was originally anonymous. The great book deserved a great name. The great name of Paul was given it. But this treatise, for it is not a letter, did not come from Paul. There is no need for alarm. We have the glory of *Hebrews* even though we know not its author. Enough is left to Paul to keep his glory undimmed.

Of the thirteen remaining letters, four are in dispute: *Ephesians*, I and II *Timothy*, and *Titus*. There is no way to determine with cool objectivity the exact authorship of this quartette of letters. Here the scholar's predilections weigh heavily in his conclusions. If he is by nature of a radical mind, he will normally tend to discard Paul's name from them. If he is naturally of a conservative mind, he will incline toward holding Paul wrote them. His views on the growth and organization of the Early Church will help direct his decision. Thus he is caught in a vicious circle. His facts not only affect his conclusions, but his outlook colors his acceptance or rejection of the facts.

Regarding these four letters, scholars take one of three positions. Some accept them outright as fully Pauline. Others with equal sureness reject them as quite non-Pauline. A third, middle-of-the-road group accepts what they call a "Pauline nucleus." They find parts in these letters that raise doubts, other parts that seem beyond question to come straight from Paul.

The ground for doubt concerning these four letters is simple but very strong. They contain, many scholars feel, descriptions of church conditions, ministerial orders, congregational organization, and community practices that belong to a time later than Paul. Also, their conception of "faith," etc., contradicts that set forth in the undisputed letters. Therefore, they say, Paul could never have written them. Others, who believe Paul did write them, declare they show that the church developed faster than the scholars who reject the letters admit. The middle-of-the-road scholars assert that some otherwise unknown writings of Paul have been worked over by later hands, but the foundations are Pauline.

In the case of *Ephesians* there is an added difficulty. In the best ancient manuscripts the word "Ephesians" does not occur. Instead there is a blank. Originally the letter probably read, "Paul, an apostle of Christ Jesus through the will of God, to the saints that are at" (space blank). If so, *Ephesians* was originally a circular letter. The blank space was purposely left so. Then when it was read in a church the name of that church could be supplied. Also, in contents *Ephesians* duplicates much in *Colossians*. Why should so busy a man as Paul write twice over on matters Colossae would surely learn from the circular letter? In *Colossians* Paul writes, "And when this epistle hath been read among you, cause that it be read also in the church of the Laodiceans." Paul was saving himself from twice writing by having *Colossians* circularized. He continues, "and that ye also read the epistle from Laodicea." That Laodicean letter is lost. But it could hardly be *Ephesians*, for Paul was plainly trying to rid himself of needless writing. And *Ephesians* largely repeats *Colossians*. So the matter ends in uncertainty.

To all this some conclusions are evident:

Paul wrote more letters than we now possess. As we shall soon see, some of his letters, as we now have them, are compiled from parts of two or more letters he wrote. They were more numerous than our New Testament would lead us to suspect.

Next, the dispute over the authenticity of certain letters ascribed to Paul is likely never to be settled. Radical and conservative minds, following their natural bents, will always disagree. Middle-of-the-road students will always abound. Agreement is impossible.

But because some scholars cannot accept these four letters as Paul's it does not follow that they throw them out of the New Testament. Far from it. While maintaining that the true author is unknown, they still recognize their lasting values.

Finally, then, we are left with nine letters everyone admits come direct from Paul: I and II *Thessalonians, Galatians,* I and II *Corinthians, Romans, Philippians, Colossians* and *Philemon.* We also have four others that may be wholly or in part Pauline: *Ephesians,* I and II *Timothy* and *Titus.*

Denying these last four letters to Paul, in no way denies the Great Apostle's glory. An author's abiding fame rests not upon how many feet of book-shelving his writings fill, but upon their enduring quality. Paul's whole correspondence, accepted and suspected together, would, in modern print, scarcely fill an ordinary-sized book of only two hundred pages. If one restricts Paul's authentic correspondence to the nine undisputed letters, they could be printed in modern fashion in not over one hundred and twenty-five pages. One slender volume only! Far less than the pages of even this small book. But how far exceeding in worth!

The *order and dating* of Paul's letters is obscure. Paul never dated his letters, nor stated specifically whence he was writing. Today this raises insoluble problems. We cannot now work out with exactness the place, time or order of his epistles. Whether *Romans* was written at Corinth, Ephesus, or elsewhere, cannot be exactly fixed. Whether *Galatians* came before or after *Colossians*, or what other letter, it is impossible to state. That *Philippians* was written from prison is clear. But whether it was written from prison at Caesarea, Rome, or more probably from one at Ephesus we can never be certain. That Paul wrote we are sure. To whom he wrote is clear. But just when and exactly whence cannot always be determined. Hence we cannot now place his letters in any sure sequence. The closely integrated schedule, long widely held, depended upon too many uncertainties and surmises to pass unchallenged.

I and II *Thessalonians* are the two writings about which we can be most sure. Clues within them plainly indicate Paul was writing during his first visit to Corinth. "We thought it good to be left behind at Athens alone; and sent Timothy . . . to comfort you concerning your faith." "Timothy came even now unto us from you, and brought us glad tidings of your faith and love." *The Acts* in relating Paul's visit to Corinth adds, "Silas and Timothy came down from Macedonia." Coming thus, they brought Paul word of the Thessalonican church. From Corinth, Paul writes to the troubled believers. Unfortunately it is not so easy to place any of Paul's other letters.

Galatians has long been considered the third of Paul's writings to his churches. At first glance this hot blast against compelling gentile Christians to keep the Mosaic law seems to dovetail neatly into the Great Council on this issue held in Jerusalem, as recorded in *The Acts* 15. Also, Paul's rapid outlining of his Gospel in *Galatians* looks like a first rough draft of his carefully developed statement in *Romans*. Unfortunately *Galatians* does not, in many essential details, fit

62

closely into *The Acts* 15. It may be that in *The Acts* Luke has followed the method adopted in his Gospel. *Mark* 6 places Jesus' tragic return to Nazareth well along in his ministry, after his work in Galilee had become widely known. But Luke, in chapter 4, moves this visit up to the beginning of Jesus' work. There it stands as a keynote to his whole ministry. Apparently in *The Acts* 15, Luke has done the same with the story of the great Jerusalem Council. Paul's struggle with the Judaizers dogged his whole ministry, as portions of the later written *Philippians* show. So Luke, as with Jesus' visit to Nazareth in his Gospel, seems to advance the Council meeting to a point early in Paul's ministry, to give his most persistent problem a more dramatic and illuminating setting.

As to *Galatians* being a rough draft of *Romans*, it may just as well be a fiery summary of Paul's widely known Gospel. Hence, *Galatians* cannot be definitely fixed, early or late, in the sequence of Paul's letters. But because the problems of the Judaizers seem to increase as Paul's ministry continued, the tendency is to believe that it belongs rather late in Paul's career. The one thing of supreme importance is, we have the letter!

The *Corinthian* correspondence is as intriguing as a detective tale. Instead of two letters, as appears on the surface, we actually have complete, or in fragments, at least four writings of Paul to the Corinthian church.

It must be remembered that neither Paul nor his churches considered his letters as sacred literature. Our Old Testament was their holy Word of God. Any letters Paul wrote his churches were kept not because they were believed to be divinely inspired, but because the church loved Paul, treasured his writings, and found in them truth worth

63

preserving. Some time after Paul's death, persons or groups, sensing the importance of Paul's writings, began collecting his letters. As they went from church to church, copying out the Pauline scrolls preserved by the local Christians, certain things were inevitable. Many of Paul's letters must have been lost entirely. Accident or carelessness destroyed them. Others were in fragments, only parts in fit condition to permit copying. Much said in one letter was repeated in another. As scrolls were expensive, and copying by hand laborious, duplicate parts were omitted; thus parts of existing letters were discarded. Again, sections of no apparent further pertinence were dropped in the copying. As the ancients did not have our modern sense of sequence and order, the copying would seem to us to be illogical and haphazard. This, in simple outline, is the story behind the rescuing of Paul's literary work. It is all well illustrated in I and II *Corinthians*.

Apparently the Corinthian correspondence had its center in Ephesus during Paul's long activity there. For while writing I *Corinthians* he says, "I will tarry at Ephesus until Pentecost." But this, our I *Corinthians*, was not Paul's first letter to that church. Already he had written them at least once. For he says "I wrote unto you in my epistle to have no company with fornicators." Here then was a letter rebuking certain sexual immoralities within the Corinthian church. That letter, the real I *Corinthians*, is lost. One can understand why the church at Corinth either did not preserve it, or later Pauline enthusiasts declined to copy it. But it is possible that we have a small fragment of it. The six verses in II *Corinthians* 6:14–7:1 interrupt the thought. Paul is writing about the glories and trials of being God's ambassador. Then suddenly, without warning, the thought breaks, and there comes the sharp rebuke, "Be not un-

equally yoked with unbelievers, . . . touch no unclean thing
. . . let us cleanse ourselves from all defilement of flesh and
spirit." Then abruptly the thought continues exactly where
it left off, upon Paul's divine ambassadorship. Why this
utterly out-of-place intrusion? The only plausible answer is
that probably we have here a small fragment of that lost
first letter to Corinthians.[1] Why this bit was preserved, and
how it got inserted in this most illogical place, we cannot
guess. But there it stands.

Next, Paul received a letter now entirely lost, from the
church at Corinth, asking him certain questions. For in our
I *Corinthians* 7:1, he says, "Now concerning the things
whereof ye wrote." And our I *Corinthians* 7–15 is taken up
in answering that letter from Corinth. Meantime, by word
of mouth he had received news directly of the unhappy
divisions in the Corinthian church: "For it has been signified unto me . . . by them . . . of Chloe, that there are contentions among you." This quarrelsome division revealed
by Chloe's people, Paul dealt with in I *Corinthians* 1–6.
Thus these two parts together compose the letter we now
know as I *Corinthians*.

In our II *Corinthians*, which was written apparently
"when we were come into Macedonia," things become
more complicated. We have just noted that part of this
letter, II *Corinthians* 6:14–7:1, is probably a fragment of
the lost letter we may call *Corinthians A*. The joyous tone
of our II *Corinthians* 1–9 is contradicted by the stern
rebukes in the later chapters of 10–13. Sensible people do
not begin letters in joyous gratitude and close them with
sharp censures. The only reasonable solution to this strange
situation is that we have here not one letter, but several

[1] Some scholars would add I *Corinthians* 6:12–20 and 10:1–22 to this
fragment, thus greatly enlarging the preserved amount of this lost letter.

65

fragments, of which the just mentioned II *Corinthians* 6:14–7:1 is one, and chapters 1–9 and 10–13 are two more. Knowing how Paul's letters were collected, this should not surprise us. Fortunately this can all be worked out quite clearly. It makes an interesting story.

The letter we know as I *Corinthians*, but which is really the second letter to Corinth, was apparently taken there by Paul's younger fellow worker, Timothy. For in our I *Corinthians* Paul writes, "For this cause have I sent unto you Timothy . . . who shall put you in remembrance of my ways." Yet Paul feared lest Timothy should be coldly received. For towards this letter's close he adds, "Now if Timothy come, see that he be with you without fear . . . let no man therefore despise him." In spite of this request, Timothy was thoroughly rebuffed. The Corinthians were in open rebellion against Paul. To meet this rebellion Paul made a hurried trip to Corinth to deal with the difficulty in person. For he writes, "This is the third time I am ready to come unto you."

But *The Acts* mentions only two visits, not three, made by Paul to Corinth: one when he first founded the church, the other just before he started on his last, fatal journey back to Jerusalem. To make that last visit "the third time" Paul must have made a visit unrecorded in *The Acts*. Evidently after Timothy's rebuff, Paul sailed directly across the Aegean from Ephesus to Corinth, tried to settle matters, then hurried back. For later in the letter he repeats, "This is the third time I am coming unto you."

This special visit to Corinth, scholars call "The Painful Visit." For later when referring back to it, Paul said, "I would not come again to you with sorrow." Or, to phrase it more clearly, 'I do not want to make you another painful visit.' This visit must have been wounding to all concerned, though Paul relied on persuasive appeal rather than castigating rebuke. This his enemies took as a sign of cowardice. Evidently quoting them, he wrote, "I who in your presence am lowly among you, but being absent am of good courage toward you." "His letters, they say, are weighty and strong; but his bodily presence is weak." In his letters, they said, he roars like a lion, but in person he purrs like a kitten. So Paul warned them, "Reckon this, that, what we are in word by letters when we are absent, such are we also in deed when we are present." Next time he would not purr, he would roar!

Before resorting to such extremes Paul wrote again, this time a strong, stern letter. Our II *Corinthians* 10–13 is the now existing fragment. Titus was delegated to deliver it to the Corinthians. "Now when I came to Troas . . . I found not Titus." He had evidently been sent with the stern letter, and for his return Paul was anxiously waiting. So Paul hurried on. "I went forth into Macedonia." There with foreboding he waited. "For even when we were come into Macedonia our flesh had no relief." Then one day Titus returned with the glad news that all was now well at Corinth. In joy Paul wrote the Corinthians how "God, comforted us by the coming of Titus . . . while he told us your longing, your mourning, your zeal for me, so that I rejoiced yet more." This joyous letter we now have in part as II *Corinthians* 1–9.[2]

This in brief outlines the Corinthian correspondence. If listed as it actually was written, it would appear thus:

1. *Corinthians* A, the case of pagan immorality, now entirely lost, except possibly the fragment in II *Corinthians* 6:14–7:1.

[2] Unless our II *Corinthians* 8–9 be considered an additional fragment of another lost letter dealing with Paul's darling project, The Collection for the poverty-stricken saints in Jerusalem. Indeed, chapters 8 and 9 could *each* be a bit from *two* such letters.

2. The letter from the Corinthians asking various questions, now entirely lost.
3. *Corinthians B* in reply to this letter, now our I *Corinthians*.
4. The hurried "painful visit" to Corinth.
5. *Corinthians C*, the letter of severe rebuke, now our II *Corinthians* 10–13.
6. *Corinthians D*, the letter of joyous relief, now our II *Corinthians* 1–9.

   (If our II *Corinthians* 8–9 be counted as one or two separate fragments on The Collection, then they should be counted as *Corinthians E*, or *Corinthians E* and *Corinthians F*.)

It becomes evident that Paul was a far busier letter-writer than the casual reader would at first suspect. "The anxiety for all the churches" entailed a most heavy and continuous burden.

Colossians, Philemon and *Ephesians*, if the latter is actually from Paul, form a trilogy. They come well along in Paul's ministry, when his work is far advanced. Formerly considered as written from Rome during his final imprisonment, many scholars now think they were written during some probable but unrecorded imprisonment in Ephesus, where Paul suffered fierce opposition during his great campaign for Christ. In *Colossians* Paul speaks of "Aristarchus my fellow prisoner." In *Philemon* he writes, "Paul, a prisoner of Christ Jesus." In *Ephesians* he is "an ambassador in chains." The arguments against this imprisonment being in Rome and for its occurring in Ephesus are many and intricate. For example, it is more reasonable to believe that the slave, Onesimus, fled not to distant Rome but to nearby Ephesus. It is hard to believe that so many of Paul's Ephesian friends, whom he mentions as being near him, should have followed him to far-off Rome. It is difficult to understand why Paul, if he were in Rome, where he was planning a mission to Spain, should write of returning to Ephesus, as he does to Philemon, requesting him to "prepare me also a lodging."

At this time Paul mentions having written a letter to the Laodiceans. Evidently, like *Colossians*, it was intended as a circular letter. "Ye also read the epistle from Laodicea." But we have no such letter. Had we this circular letter, we should know it as the *Epistle to the Laodiceans*. What has become of it? Some scholars think our *Philemon* is that letter. But it is so personal and individual as to make such a conclusion almost preposterous. Others think that our present *Ephesians*, another circular letter, is the lost *Laodiceans*. But it is so much like *Colossians*, it is hard to believe it constitutes the lost letter to Laodicea. Besides, *Ephesians* is, on other grounds, thought by many to be non-Pauline. It is quite probable that *Laodiceans* is forever lost. Suffice it that we have two of these beautiful letters—*Colossians* and *Philemon*—from Paul quite undisputed, and perhaps a third in *Ephesians*. Thus late in his missionary career, while in bonds "the anxiety for all the churches" pressed heavily upon him, adding to his weariness in his sufferings.

Philippians, as has been suggested, is most probably fragments of two letters. Chapters 1–3:1, with 4:8–23, make a sort of *Philippians* A, written to thank the church at Philippi for their gift of money. Chapters 3:2–4:7 compose a kind of *Philippians* B, warning the church sharply of the Judaizing menace. Where and when the second of these fragments was written cannot now be surmised. The letter of gratitude was written while Paul was in prison. He speaks warmly of "they that are of Caesar's household." This phrase could suggest connections with the government in Rome. Once in Rome, Paul had planned to continue west to Spain. But here in *Philippians* he is planning to return to Philippi once more. "I trust in the Lord that I myself also shall come shortly." This makes it difficult to fit *Philippians* into Paul's Roman imprisonment. This reference to Caesar's household can just as well refer to government officials in Ephesus. If so, then this word of thanks was penned during an unrecorded arrest in Ephesus, and the letter belongs with *Colossians* and *Philemon*. In any case Paul, though imprisoned, was busy overseeing the affairs of his beloved churches.

Romans, Paul tells us, was written at the close of his missionary activities in the cities surrounding the Aegean Sea. "Wherefore also I was hindered these many times from coming to you: but now, having no more any place in these regions, and having these many years a longing to come unto you, whensoever I go unto Spain, for I hope to see you in my journey. . . . But now . . . I go unto Jerusalem, ministering unto the saints . . . to make a certain contribution for the poor . . . that are at Jerusalem." "When therefore I have accomplished this . . . I will go on by you into Spain." The letter is plainly written to introduce his Gospel as he preached it to a church he did not found, whose members were strangers to him, and to whom he wished to explain his plans for carrying the Gospel to Spain. So without the usual personal greetings, for he knew few if any Christians in Rome, the letter closes at the end of chapter 15 with an appropriate benediction.

Then comes the surprise of chapter 16, with its "I commend unto you Phoebe our sister, who is a servant of the church that is at Cenchreae: that ye receive her in the Lord." Then, surprisingly enough, follows a list of twenty-six names to whom Paul desires to be remembered. "Salute Prisca and Aquila," and twenty-four named. "Salute" is repeated eighteen times. It is equivalent to our 'Remember me to ——.'

But Paul knew practically no one in Rome. This large group of friends could hardly have preceded him there. What do these names mean? The solution seems plain enough. In that day Christians could not afford in their travels to put up at inns. Often, too, these inns were unclean places of ill repute. Therefore they sought out and were welcomed into the homes of fellow Christians. As surety of their character and Christian faith, and to prevent fraud, they carried with them letters of introduction. This sixteenth chapter, except for its concluding benediction, is such a letter of introduction. Many of the names, we learn from other letters of Paul, belonged to people in Ephesus. Here, then, is plainly a letter written by Paul, perhaps from Corinth, to friends in Ephesus, commending Phoebe's Christian character, and requesting that "ye assist her in whatsoever matter she may have need." So we add to our list of Paul's writings this little note of introduction.

I and II *Timothy*, and *Titus*, as we have seen, are suspected by many scholars as not being fully Pauline. They think much in them belongs to a time later than Paul. Nor can they be fitted into any scheme of Paul's intended movements.

I *Timothy* does not state where Paul is. Its late atmosphere points directly to Rome. But contrarily, the phrase, "when I was going into Macedonia," suggests Philippi. It shows Paul to be free, or soon expecting to be free and able to travel. "These things I write unto thee, hoping to come unto thee shortly." "Till I come, give heed unto reading."

In *Titus* Paul has left Rome. But instead of heading west toward Spain, as he had planned, he has turned east once more. He has evangelized in Crete, where so far as *The Acts* shows, he had never before preached. And he intended to winter in northwest Greece at Nicopolis. "For this cause," he writes to Titus, who apparently was on the island, "left I thee in Crete." "Give diligence to come unto me to Nicopolis: for there I have determined to winter."

In II *Timothy* Paul is imprisoned in Rome and facing immediate martyrdom. "Onesiphorus . . . was not ashamed of my . . . chain . . . when he was in Rome." But others were not so loyal. "At my first defence no one took my part, but all forsook me." "The time of my departure is come."

All this is most confusing. *The Acts* left Paul under house-arrest, but free to preach. In *Romans* Paul was planning to visit Spain. Here, instead of carrying out his plans, he is back again among his Aegean churches. If there is a nucleus of genuine Pauline authenticity in these three letters, something we need to know to straighten out this puzzle is missing.

The last we see of Paul in his letters, his doom is sure, though his heart is unbowed. For the great paean of II *Timothy*, "I am already being offered," sounds authentically Pauline. He is facing the moment when he can "depart and be with Christ."

This summary of the form, method, purpose and order of Paul's letters reveals the surprising fact that we do not have, as appears, thirteen straight-out epistles. Nor do we have a supposed nine authentic and four doubtful writings. Instead, we have a far richer and more varied correspondence.

We possess at least seven complete, undisputed letters:

1. I Thessalonians.
2. II Thessalonians.
3. Galatians.

72

4. I Corinthians.
5. Philemon.
6. Romans 1–15.
7. Colossians.

We have also the fragments of some six authentic letters:

8. II Corinthians 6:14–7:1, the rebuke to pagan immorality.
9. II Corinthians 10–13, the stern letter.
10. II Corinthians 1–9, the joyous letter.
11. Philippians 1–3:1 with 4:8–23, the letter of thanks.
12. Philippians 3:2–4:7, warning against Judaizers.
13. Romans 16:1–24, introducing Phoebe to the Ephesian church.

Further, we possess the four disputed works:

14. Ephesians.
15. I Timothy.
16. Titus.
17. II Timothy; this letter especially seems to possess a strong Pauline nucleus recording his triumphant facing of martyrdom.

Finally, we learn of one letter Paul mentions as having written, the now lost *Laodiceans*.

Here we possess in whole or in part, thirteen genuine Pauline letters. If our II Corinthians 8–9 be counted as two separate fragments on "The Collection," we have a possible fifteen unquestioned writings by Paul. In addition we know of the lost letter to the *Laodiceans*. We have, also, the four disputed works which may be in part authentically Pauline. Thus does the analysis of Paul's letters reveal their surprising number!

The *value* of Paul's letters, in spite of the perplexing confusion such an analysis at first creates, is greatly enlarged

73

and enriched. Our knowledge of the great apostle is vastly clarified and increased. The number of his letters was far greater, the travel back and forth by friends and personal representatives, by messengers bearing news and gifts, and by Paul himself was far more frequent than we would otherwise surmise.

Moreover, this rapid survey, broad as it is, discloses a Paul who endured labors, hardships and sufferings far more severe and numerous than his journeys as recorded in *The Acts* unfold. He made trips and visited places the rapid narrative in *The Acts* could not linger to relate. There are, for example, his many beatings, his oft imprisonments, his tenacious clinging to his many friends, and his continual buffetings by the unwearied Judaizers. There is, too, his quick special trip across the Aegean to Corinth from Ephesus and back again, as revealed in II *Corinthians*. There is, as shown in *Romans*, an otherwise unknown preaching mission through the Illyricum territory, a region northwest of modern Greece and roughly corresponding to present-day Albania. There is the bare possibility of his wintering in western Greece, on the eastern shore of the Adriatic at Nicopolis, as stated in *Titus*.

By this tedious analysis, these and a hundred other lesser details come to light through these possible dozen and a half writings of the Great Apostle.

The profound thought that Paul poured into his letters is also invaluably enriched. We can now get the letters into some kind of order, and lay out their main points in better fashion. We can see more clearly precisely what Paul was thinking and why. It is their profound thought and Christian instruction that gives to Paul's letters their eternal value. To an outline of their points we must now turn our attention.

Chapter 6

THE PASTOR TEACHER

His Letters: Their Contents

"I think that I also have the Spirit of God."

PAUL WROTE for very ordinary people. For the most part they were men and women of little or no education. They were humble artisans, toiling manual laborers, and hard-driven slaves. "Not many wise," as Paul learned, yielded to the Gospel message. What he wrote needed phrasing so it could be readily grasped by untrained minds. The main points of his letters even today are usually quite clear. There are digressions and obscurities, but the essential points are plainly stated. They can be quickly discovered by any ordinary modern reader who will apply himself.

I *Thessalonians* was written chiefly to correct some misunderstandings regarding Christ's Second Coming. Paul being "at Athens alone" had "sent Timothy, our brother . . . to establish you . . . concerning your faith; that no man be moved by these afflictions." And Timothy having gone to Thessalonica to encourage the persecuted believers, "came even now unto us" at Corinth, "and brought us glad tidings of your faith and love." The Thessalonians were holding firm in the face of suffering. So Paul encourages them to continue. "Ye ought to walk and to please God," "For God called us not for uncleanness, but in sanctification." Then

75

Paul turns to the matter they evidently had asked Timothy to lay before him. "We would not have you ignorant, brethren, concerning them that fall asleep." Plainly some of the saints in the little Thessalonican church had died. Would they share in the glories of Christ's appearing, or be left behind? So Paul explains, "The Lord himself shall descend from heaven . . . and the dead in Christ shall rise first; then we that are alive . . . shall together with them be caught up . . . to meet the Lord in the air: and so shall we ever be with the Lord." Since this "day of the Lord so cometh as a thief in the night," "let us not sleep . . . but let us watch and be sober." This, then, is the message, simple but profound: 'Continue to endure, walk as to please God; all of us alive and dead shall share together the glory of Christ's appearing, so let us be alert and earnest.' Even ordinary people could not misunderstand that.

Yet II *Thessalonians* shows that some did. Some of those manual laborers, it is correctly inferred from what Paul wrote, were saying, 'Well, if the Lord is coming soon, there's no need of our working and saving up for a rainy day and for old age.' So they threw down their tools. Being idle, they promptly fell into the leisure-time mischiefs of mean gossip and low vice. This Timothy evidently reported to Paul upon his return. Paul had to clear matters up with a second letter. "We are bound to give thanks to God always for you, . . . for your patience and faith in all your persecutions and in the afflictions which ye endure." The little church was bravely holding out. "Now . . . touching the coming of our Lord Jesus Christ, . . . that ye be not quickly shaken from your mind . . . by epistle as from us, as that day of the Lord is just at hand; except the falling away come *first*, and the man of sin be revealed." Evidently

76

though the Lord was coming, and Paul himself expected to witness this wonder, some time must yet elapse before it would come to pass. Only "then shall be revealed the lawless one, whom the Lord Jesus shall slay." Therefore, "in the name of our Lord Jesus Christ, . . . withdraw yourselves from every brother that walketh disorderly," "If any will not work, neither let him eat. For we hear of some that . . . are busybodies. Now them that are such we commend . . . that with quietness they work, and eat their own bread." That is: 'Continue your enduring courage, do not expect Christ's appearing immediately, stop loafing and gossiping and go to work.' And the humblest day-laborer understood!

Galatians concerns the very different matter of the Christian's freedom from the shackles of the Mosaic Law. Among Paul's Asia Minor converts a heated controversy flamed. Certain Christian Jews, brought up in the strict observance of the Mosaic rituals, insisted that the old Law was God-given and still binding. Jesus did not cancel it, they said, he merely set a capstone upon it. Gentiles who accepted Christ, if they expected to be admitted to the fellowship of Christian Jews, must accept the Mosaic Law. They must be circumcised, observe the Jewish food taboos, keep the stated feasts and fasts, and obey all the other scriptural regulations. The Jewish Christians holding these convictions are known as "Judaizers."

Paul, on the contrary, believed that Christ's coming cancelled these restrictions. Because Christ had superseded the Law, Paul declared that all gentiles were freed from these Jewish ritual observances. Salvation was given only through Christ, and apart from the Law. His opponents replied by spreading the libel that Paul, because of his late conversion, was no true apostle. He had picked up his message from the Jerusalem apostles second hand, as bread crumbs thrown to birds. Then they went on to cite scripture to prove, as they believed, that all gentiles must accept the Mosaic Law in full, or forfeit their Christian fellowship.

Galatians is Paul's reply. It is smoking hot. "Though we or an angel from heaven should preach unto you any gospel other than that which we preached unto you, let him be anathema." 'Damned!' we would say. Then Paul defends his apostolic calling. As for "the gospel which was preached by me . . . neither did I receive it from man, nor was I taught it, but it came to me through revelation of Jesus Christ." "It was the good pleasure of God . . . to reveal his Son in me." Not only had the brethren at Jerusalem not taught him his message, they had approved his preaching to the gentiles freedom from the Law. "Not even Titus, . . . being a Greek, was compelled to be circumcised," "but contrariwise," Peter, James and John, "when they saw that I had been intrusted with the gospel of the uncircumcision . . . gave to me and Barnabas the right hands of fellowship, that we should go unto the Gentiles."

By their own experience the Galatian believers could, themselves, testify to this truth that the Spirit was a gift received by faith, not by the work of the Law. "Received ye the Spirit by the works of the law, or by the hearing of faith?" It was by the hearing of faith. The scriptures showed this was the only true way. Abraham had been saved, not by the Law but by faith. "Abraham believed God, and it was reckoned unto him for righteousness. . . . The righteous shall live by faith." So "for freedom did Christ set us free." "If ye receive circumcision, Christ will profit you nothing. . . . For in Christ Jesus neither circumcision availeth anything, nor uncircumcision; but faith working through love."

Therefore, "Walk by the Spirit, and ye shall not fulfil the lust of the flesh."

That is the gist of *Galatians*: 'There is no other gospel than the gospel of salvation by faith which I received by revelation, which the Jerusalem church approved, which you experienced by faith, which began with Abraham, which if you abandon will cancel your salvation in Christ, and which empowers you to walk in the Spirit.' No one has ever been able to refute this burning argument.

We now come to the Corinthian correspondence. This must be followed through as outlined in the last chapter.

Corinthians A was a letter rebuking the church for too close association with pagan immoral practices. Only the fragment found in our II *Corinthians* 6:14–7:1 now remains. "Be ye not unequally yoked with unbelievers . . . what portion hath a believer with an unbeliever? . . . let us cleanse ourselves from all defilement of flesh and spirit." Paul would never countenance any accord between Belial and Christ.

Corinthians B, which we know as I *Corinthians*, seeks to correct some abuses endangering the church at Corinth, and answer some questions sent to Paul in a letter, now lost. Also some members of the "household of Chloe" had come from Corinth to Paul at Ephesus, bringing word of unseemly practices rife in the Corinthian church. "For it hath been signified unto me . . . by them that are of the household of Chloe, that there are contentions among you." At the time, Paul was engrossed in his Ephesian mission so that a visit to Corinth to clear up matters was impossible. "I will tarry at Ephesus until Pentecost; for a great door and effectual is opened unto me, and there are many adversaries."

Paul begins his letter with the abuses which endanger the Corinthian church. First, there are factions (chaps. 1–4). The poor little church was split four ways. "Each one of you saith, I am of Paul; and I of Apollos; and I of Cephas; and I of Christ." Even early preachers differed in style and emphasis. Some Corinthians apparently preferred the rugged style of Peter. Besides, he was an "original" disciple. Some liked best the fluent oratory of the Alexandrian Apollos. Others clung with tenacious loyalty to Paul, their church's founder. But a few, deploring the whole sad business, stood neutral under the slogan, "I of Christ." Pride was in part the origin of this division. Each group thought it possessed a better brand of the Gospel. Such supposed "wisdom," Paul answered, was nonsense. For "God chose the foolish things of the world, that he might put to shame them that are wise," "For the kingdom of God is not in word, but in power." As for Peter, Paul and Apollos, the Corinthians owed their loyalty to Christ alone. "Other foundation can no man lay than that which is laid, which is Jesus Christ."

Next, a case of incest (chap. 5). "One of you hath his father's wife." Worse, nothing was being done about it. Paul's orders were peremptory. Excommunicate the offender. "Deliver such a one unto Satan for the destruction of the flesh." That might shock him and save his soul, "that the spirit may be saved in the day of the Lord."

Lawsuits were the next unchristian practice to receive Paul's stern judgment (chap. 6:1–8). "Dare any of you, having a matter against his neighbor, go to law before the unrighteous, and not before the saints?" The fact that these lawsuits occurred witnessed their failure as Christians. "It is altogether a defect in you, that ye have lawsuits one with another." Such disputes should never be taken before pagan gentile courts, with their pagan standards. Let the church settle them by Christian principles. Better still, never press a dispute. "Why not rather take wrong? why not rather be defrauded?" Anything, even to suffering injustice, than to be quarreling Christians before the world!

Immorality was another vice lurking within the Corinthian church (chap. 6:9–20). Against its many forms Paul warns: "Neither fornicators, nor idolators, nor adulterers, nor effeminate, nor abusers of themselves with men, nor thieves, nor covetous, nor drunkards, nor revilers, nor extortioners, shall inherit the kingdom of God." A lofty view of one's personal physical sacredness offered the cure. "Know ye not that your body is a temple of the Holy Spirit which is in you, which ye have from God? and ye are not your own; for ye were bought with a price: glorify God therefore in your body."

Paul now turns to the questions raised in the letter from the Corinthian Christians.

First, is it advisable for a church member to marry? (chap. 7). One by one Paul takes up the various marital states. Let those unable to exercise sexual self-control be married. "Because of fornications, let each man have his own wife, and let each woman have her own husband." As to virgins and widows, if possible let them remain single. "It is good for them if they abide even as I. But if they have not continency, let them marry." As to the married, let them not be separated. Let "the wife depart not from her husband," let "the husband leave not his wife." As for the Christian husband or wife married to an unbeliever, let them not separate unless the unbeliever demands it. "For how knowest thou . . . whether thou shalt save thy" partner? Paul's reasons for preferring celibacy, while permitting marriage, were two. The swiftly expected return of the Lord made marriage of no importance. Also, "He that is unmarried is careful for the things of the Lord, how he may please the Lord: but he that is married is careful for the things of the world, how he may please his wife, and is divided." To "please the Lord" must ever be the believer's first desire.

Next, are Christians free to eat meat which pagans have first offered to idols? (chaps. 8–10). In that day men really believed in "demons," invisible spirits, and in the reality of idols. Idols were a spiritual force rivaling the one true God. Pagans were accustomed to offer a sacrifice to one of their gods, and with the meat of the victim give a feast to their friends, in honor of the god. Sometimes they invited their Christian friends. What should Christians do? Some said, 'Go and enjoy yourself,' for "no idol is anything in the world, and . . . there is no God but one." Others drew back lest such participation be a recognition of the idol and its spirit. What should be done? "Now concerning things sacrificed to idols. . . . Knowledge puffeth up, but love edifieth." One was free to exercise one's liberty and go to the banquet. "But take heed lest by any means this liberty of yours become a stumbling block to the weak. . . . For through thy knowledge he that is weak perisheth, the brother for whose sake Christ died." "All things are lawful; but not all things are expedient. . . . Let no man seek his own, but each his neighbor's good." "Whether therefore ye eat, or drink, . . . do all to the glory of God. Give no occasion of stumbling, . . . seeking . . . the profit of the many."

The social convention of women being veiled in public is Paul's next topic (chap. 11:2–16). Should Christian women, freed from the Mosaic Law, be compelled to keep such pagan social conventions as going about veiled? Could they not exercise their freedom and be rid of the inconvenience? Paul passes by the scandal such a practice would stir up. That Christian women would at once be taken for immoral street-walkers was too obvious to need comment. He forbids the suggestion on, to him, the valid grounds of the order of creation. Christian women should keep the veil as an evidence of male supremacy. So God had created things. "The head of every man is Christ; and the head of the woman is the man; and the head of Christ is God." God, Christ, man, woman: that to Paul was the divine order of Creation. "For this cause ought the woman to have a sign of authority on her head." Even social custom should express the divine order.

In his next topic, Paul turned to questions growing out of scandals in the observance of the Lord's Supper (chap. 11:17–34). In that day the Supper was a real meal, during which was observed the bread and wine memorial. Some came early and ate and drank more than their share. Late-comers found little food left, and some of the early participants "drunken." No fellowship with Christ or with one another was possible. The cure was obvious. Give heed to the meaning of the Supper, and to one's own self. "For as often as ye eat this bread, and drink the cup, ye proclaim the Lord's death till he come. Wherefore whosoever shall eat the bread or drink the cup of the Lord in an unworthy manner, shall be guilty of the body and blood of the Lord. But let a man prove himself, and so let him eat of the bread, and drink of the cup. . . . Wherefore, my brethren, when ye come together to eat, wait one for another."

Continuing, Paul answers the troublesome problem: Which are the chief spiritual gifts? (chaps. 12–14). The Corinthians were evidently envious of each other. They

83

gave preference to showy abilities, especially to the noisy "speaking with tongues." This was most probably the joyous, inarticulate shouting of Christians in their meetings.[1] It was a gift highly prized in Corinth. But it made for mere noise, disorder, jealousy and misplaced emphasis. "Now," said Paul, "there are diversities of gifts, but the same Spirit. . . . but all these worketh the one and the same Spirit, dividing to each one severally even as he will." The thing to do is to "desire earnestly the greater gifts" of faith, hope and love, the only three gifts that last on. All others eventually vanish. Therefore especially "Follow after love; yet desire earnestly spiritual gifts." As for tongues, "If any man speaketh in a tongue . . . let one interpret: but if there be no interpreter, let him keep silence." "Let all things be done decently and in order."

The last question the Corinthians asked Paul concerned the Resurrection (chap. 15). One group was declaring Jesus could not have risen from the dead. To some this was a miracle utterly impossible. Another group, following their Greek way of thinking and not accustomed to Jewish thought, asserted that in their immortal state men possessed no body, but were pure spirits. To the first group, Paul replies "that Christ died for our sins . . . he was buried; and that he hath been raised on the third day." Then citing his proof, he declares, "if Christ hath not been raised, your faith is vain; ye are yet in your sins. . . . But now hath Christ been raised from the dead, the first fruits of them that are asleep." As for those who said, "How are the dead raised? and with what manner of body do they come?" Paul answers, "God giveth it a body even as it pleased him."

[1] Moffatt in his *N. T. Commentary* on I *Cor.*, p. 208, describes them as "Broken murmurs, incoherent chants, low mutterings, *staccato* sobs, screams, and sighs, dropped from the speakers' lips in hurried, huddled utterances."

About the exact nature of this risen body he does not speculate. "If there is a natural body, there is also a spiritual body . . . thanks be to God, who giveth us the victory through our Lord Jesus Christ."

Lastly, Paul takes up a concern of his own (chap. 16). "Now concerning the collection for the saints. . . . Upon the first day of the week let each one of you lay by him in store, as he may prosper. . . . And when I arrive, whomsoever ye shall approve, them will I send with letters to carry your bounty unto Jerusalem." "Let all that ye do be done in love."

A long, varied letter is *Corinthians B*. Ancient though much of its matter is, it is rich in questions and principles that have continually troubled Christ's church.

Corinthians C, which to us is II *Corinthians* 10–13, is a letter of severe rebuke. Many charges against himself Paul repeats. He was labeled as "lowly" in bearing, having a boastful "courage" that covered an inner cowardice, he "walked according to the flesh," was full of "imaginations," boasted unseemly that "he is Christ's," "glorying" in his "authority," he tried to "terrify" by his letters, he was "rude in speech," "bold," could "lie," was "foolish," and being "nothing," was a nobody. Paul's answers asserted his superiority of inheritance, being "of the seed of Abraham"; his superiority in missionary effort and sufferings, "in labors more abundantly"; and his superiority in revelations, "caught up even to the third heaven." And now "this is the third time I am coming to you." If the Corinthians have not repented, it will be necessary to take stern measures. "If I come again, I will not spare." But he hoped for a change of heart in them. "That I may not when present deal sharply." Always Paul hoped for peace.

Corinthians D, a letter of joyous relief that things are again well between him and the Christians at Corinth, we know as II *Corinthians* 1–9. His enemies, again on his trail, had charged him with "fickleness," saying one thing and doing another, having lordship over his converts, "corrupting the word of God" by not binding the Mosaic Law upon his gentile converts, "commending" himself instead of presenting letters of recommendation from the Jerusalem authorities, making a blustering show of courage to cover his cowardice, "walking according to the flesh," "handling the word of God deceitfully," preaching himself, being "beside" himself, a "deceiver" and "unknown."

Paul replied that his fickleness was only an unexpected change of plans. He could not keep his word about returning to Corinth until differences had been settled, lest he seem to abet the charge of "lordship." "To spare you I forbare to come unto Corinth." As to "corrupting the word of God" and "commending" himself, they had ample evidence of the sincerity of his ministry. Its success was witnessed by his converts, who were his real letters of recommendation. "Ye are our epistle . . . read of all men." Its abiding glory exceeded the passing glory of the Law. "The children of Israel could not look stedfastly upon the face of Moses for the glory of his face; which glory was passing away." "But we all, with unveiled face beholding as in a mirror the glory of the Lord, are transformed into the same image from glory to glory, even as from the Lord the Spirit." Its hope is the glory of immortality. "For we know that if the earthly house of our tabernacle be dissolved, we have a building from God, a house not made with hands, eternal, in the heavens." Its motive is that "the love of Christ constraineth us" for "we are ambassadors therefore on behalf of Christ." Its work involves enduring terrible sufferings "as having nothing, and yet possessing all things."

But now the trouble was over. Paul was comforted "by the coming of Titus" whom he had sent to correct matters at Corinth, who told Paul of "your longing, your mourning, your zeal for me; so that I rejoiced yet more." The Corinthian difficulty was past.

Chapters 8 and 9 of this letter deal with Paul's great project, the Collection for the Jerusalem saints. Evidently the Corinthian church was cool. Never using the word 'money,' but calling this benevolence "this liberality," "this grace," "ministry," "abundance," "bounty," "proof of love," "service," and "contribution," Paul urges the Corinthians to give "not grudgingly, or of necessity: for God loveth a cheerful giver," and reminds them "of the exceeding grace of God in you. Thanks be to God for his unspeakable gift."

With this call to benevolence, which, as we have seen, may be *Corinthians E*, or *E* and *F*, the long correspondence with the Corinthian Christians ends.

Romans 1–15 is the only letter Paul wrote to a church he did not found. He was hoping to visit Rome, "having these many years a longing to come unto you . . . but now . . . I go unto Jerusalem, ministering unto the saints . . . when therefore I have accomplished this . . . I will go on by you unto Spain." Never having been in Rome, Paul could not deal with local concerns of the church there. His object was to outline his Gospel, that it might be familiar to the membership when he arrived.

"I am not ashamed of the gospel: for it is the power of God unto salvation to everyone that believeth." Men need this salvation, "for the wrath of God is revealed from heaven against all ungodliness." This salvation is provided "through faith in Jesus Christ unto all them that believe." Having received this salvation we are "justified by faith," and "have peace with God through our Lord Jesus Christ; through whom also . . . we rejoice in hope of the glory of God." It was the knowledge of the Law that brought a sense of sin, for "I had not known sin, except through the law." But now having obtained salvation through faith in Christ, "There is therefore now no condemnation to them that are in Christ Jesus . . . but ye received the spirit of adoption, whereby we cry, Abba, Father. . . . we are children of God: and if children, then heirs; heirs of God, and joint-heirs with Christ." As for the Jews who possessed the Law, but have rejected Christ, "Did God cast off his people? God forbid. . . . They also, if they continue not in their unbelief, shall be grafted in . . . and so all Israel shall be saved." Having received this great salvation "by the mercies of God, . . . present your bodies a living sacrifice, holy, acceptable to God, which is your spiritual service." "Owe no man anything, save to love one another."

This in outline, which will receive further explanation in a later chapter, is the gist of Paul's Gospel.

Romans 16 constitutes a little note, introducing Phoebe to the Ephesian Christians. "I commend unto you Phoebe our sister, who is a servant of the church that is at Cenchreae." Then follow more than a score of names, fellow Christians to whom Paul wished to be remembered. Paul never forgot a friend.

Colossians was written to exalt the supremacy of Christ. Some of the Colossians were falling into the error of equating, if not subordinating Christ to invisible, angelic spirits in whom they believed and sometimes worshipped. These spirits they called by such vague names as "thrones," "dominions," and "powers." They also emphasized the necessity of special sabbaths, feast and fast days, and abstaining from specified foods. Altogether, they made Jesus' religion weird, complicated, half-superstitious, ascetic, and practicable only to those especially favored.

Paul answered by exalting Christ to divine supremacy in all things. He "is the image of the invisible God, the first-born of all creation . . . he is before all things, and in him all things consist . . . that in all things he might have the pre-eminence." Therefore let the Colossians "take heed lest there shall be any one that maketh spoil of you through his philosophy and vain deceit," for in Christ "dwelleth all the fulness of the Godhead bodily." As for food restrictions, feast days and other arbitrary observances, "Let no man therefore judge you in meat, or in drink, or in respect of a feast day, or a new moon or a sabbath," or "worshipping of the angels." Finally, in view of Christ's glory, "Put on therefore, as God's elect, . . . a heart of compassion, kindness, lowliness, . . . forbearing one another," knowing that "Christ is all, and in all."

Philippians A is a letter of joyous gratitude to the Christians at Philippi for a gift of money he received from them. We know it as *Philippians* 1–3:1 with 4:8–23. After his customary greetings and prayers, Paul declares that his imprisonment, rather than hindering the progress of the Gospel, was promoting it. "I would have you know, brethren, that the things which happened unto me have fallen out rather unto the progress of the gospel; so that my bonds became manifest in Christ throughout the whole praetorian guard, and to all the rest." Therefore, the Philippians can take courage when evil days fall on them. "Stand fast in one spirit, . . . and in nothing affrighted by the adversaries." Such endurance should remind them of the sufferings of Christ Jesus, "who, existing in the form of God, counted not the being on an equality with God a thing to be grasped, but emptied himself, taking the form of a servant, being made in the likeness of men; . . . he humbled himself . . . even unto . . . the death of the cross. Wherefore also God highly exalted him." As for the future, "I trust in the Lord that I myself [being released] shall come shortly." So, "Finally, my brethren, rejoice in the Lord." Then, following a second "finally," Paul gives thanks for the Philippian gift. "I rejoice in the Lord greatly, that now at length ye have revived your thought for me." "Ye did well that ye had fellowship with my affliction." Paul obeyed his own injunction "in everything give thanks."

Philippians B, so to call the irrelevant section of our *Philippians* 3:2–4:7, blasts at the Judaizers who were ever persecuting Paul and undoing his work. "Beware of the dogs." Stern words, but Paul could not bear to see his Christian converts jeopardized. All return by any of them to the rudiments of the Law would be fatal. "Beware of the concision . . . have no confidence in the flesh." I, Paul, know whereof I speak, for I was "circumcised the eighth day, . . . as touching the law, a Pharisee . . . as touching the righteousness which is in the law, found blameless. Howbeit . . . these have I counted loss for Christ . . . not having a righteousness . . . which is of the law, but that . . . which is from God by faith." Those who teach slavery to the Law are "enemies of the cross of Christ: whose end is perdition." To return to the thraldom of the Law meant for Paul the surrender of the Cross, and the denial of Christ, who to him was over all and all in all.

Philemon is a simple, personal note, occupying but a single page. It contains neither teaching nor doctrine. Paul, still in prison, requests that Philemon, his wealthy convert at Colossae, receive back with Christian grace one Onesimus, a slave who apparently had robbed Philemon and run away. For Paul writes that if he "oweth thee aught, put that to mine account." Somehow Onesimus had met Paul, become converted, and now, though Paul's son in the Gospel, Paul was sending him back. Would Philemon receive him, not only as his legal slave, but as Paul's son in faith, and a Christian brother? As for the stolen property, if Philemon insisted, though he owed Paul his life in Christ, Paul would himself make it up.

A one-page note, but one of the most gracious and beautiful personal communications in all literature.

This ends the summary of the occasion and contents of Paul's undisputed letters. A further summary of the disputed letters is now in order.

Ephesians, as we have learned, was originally a circular letter. Its theme is the exaltation of Christ, and the unity of mankind in him, through the church. God's great purpose is "to sum up all things in Christ, the things in the heavens, and the things upon the earth," and make "him to be head over all things to the church, which is his body, the fulness of him that filleth all in all."

Into these riches of spiritual glory the Asia Minor gentiles have been admitted. For now you who "were dead through your trespasses and sins" did "God, being rich in mercy" make alive together with Christ . . . that in the ages to come he might show the exceeding riches of his grace in kindness toward us in Christ Jesus." "So then ye are no more strangers and sojourners, but ye are fellow-citizens with the saints, and of the household [church] of God," "to the intent that now unto the principalities and the powers in the heavenly places might be made known through the church the manifold wisdom of God."

It is by faith in Christ operating through the church that the divisions of mankind will be unified. "There is one body, [the church] and one Spirit, even as also ye were called in one hope of your calling; one Lord, one faith, one baptism, one God and father of all, who is over all, and through all, and in all."

Therefore, give "diligence to keep the unity," "no longer walk as the Gentiles," but "put on the new man." Keep Christ-like all life's relationships as husbands, wives, children and slaves. Finally, "Be strong in the Lord," "Put on the whole armor of God," and "Grace be with all."

I *Timothy* records Paul's directions to his young understudy and trusted assistant. Timothy was the son of a Greek father and a Jewish mother, Eunice. He had been converted during one of Paul's journeys through Asia Minor. As Paul's companion and fellow worker, he had, for example, carried some of the Corinthian letters, and acted in Corinth as Paul's deputy.

In this letter the aging Paul writes Timothy advice on his personal conduct, and his administering of the churches. He is to cling fast to the pure Gospel, and see that others do likewise. "I exhorted thee . . . that thou mightest charge certain men not to teach a different doctrine." "This charge I commit unto thee" that thou shouldst hold the "faith and a good conscience; which some having thrust from them made shipwreck concerning the faith." "I exhort therefore, . . . that supplication, prayers, intercessions, thanksgivings, be made for all men." "I desire therefore that the men pray in every place, . . . that women adorn themselves in modest apparel." Thus is Timothy to maintain the faith, and keep order in worship.

Then follows a long succession of practical admonitions on the qualifications of church officials and members, bishops, deacons, women, widows, elders, servants and the rich. Advice is also given concerning his own personal conduct toward the elders, youths, elderly women, girls and widows.

Finally, "Fight the good fight of the faith, lay hold on the life eternal," and "guard the deposit [of faith] which is committed unto thee."

Titus is the least valuable of all the letters credited to Paul. This word to his co-worker, who accompanied him on many a journey, purports to have left Titus in Crete, an island on which we have no record of Paul's having conducted any missionary campaign.

First, Paul reminds Titus that the Cretans are, to quote one of their own number, "liars, evil beasts, idle gluttons. This testimony," Paul adds, "is true." Titus, therefore, is to "reprove them sharply."

Then follows, as in I and II *Timothy*, an extended series of admonitions concerning Titus himself, aged men and women, young women and men, "in all things showing thyself an ensample of good works." Before these under his charge he is so to live "that the word of God be not blasphemed," and "that they may adorn the doctrine of God our Saviour in all things."

II *Timothy* is in the heroic mood. Paul is in chains, expecting shortly to be martyred. Hence the repeated call to

Timothy to "suffer hardship." "Suffer hardship with the gospel according to the power of God." Whoever so suffers hardship will never be put to shame. For in his bonds Paul explains, "I am not ashamed; for I know him whom I have believed . . . that he is able to guard that which I have committed unto him." Others have been courageous in face of Paul's arrest, for "Onesiphorus . . . oft refreshed me, and was not ashamed of my chain." "Thou therefore, my child, be strengthened in the grace that is in Christ Jesus." So, "suffer hardship with me, as a good soldier of Christ Jesus." "Remember Jesus Christ, risen from the dead . . . according to my gospel: wherein I suffer hardship unto bonds." "Yea, and all that would live godly in Christ Jesus shall suffer persecution." "Suffer hardship, do the work of an evangelist, fulfil thy ministry."

Then comes the grand valedictory. "I am already being offered, and the time of my departure is come. I have fought the good fight, I have finished the course, I have kept the faith: henceforth there is laid up for me the crown of righteousness."

On this high note of ringing confidence the Pauline correspondence ends.

This analysis of the main points in Paul's letters has probably dismayed the reader. It is dull and unexciting, as all such analyses must be. But worse, the very ideas themselves may seem quite commonplace, and without exciting challenge. Little in this chapter, as the introduction on *The Importance of Paul* has stated, would turn Augustine to the good life, stir Luther to reinvigorate all Christendom, warm Wesley's heart, or jolt modern westernism out of its easy optimism. Little appears here sufficient to make Paul's letters truth to set the heart afire, stir profound theological argument, develop enriched spiritual insight, and both convict and convince the world "concerning the faith in Christ Jesus . . . righteousness, and self-control, and the judgment to come." Here there seems to be little more than commonplace conclusions on the obvious.

The reasons for this are three. First, what may now appear to us as trite truth, in Paul's day was new and revolutionary. Second, the main points of Paul's letters, so swiftly outlined here, cannot do justice to the deeper wealth of Paul's mind. No outline can disclose the riches of a great thinker. It is the *principles that underlie the outlined points* that give thought its wealth of meaning. With Paul, it is what his points imply and how they are developed that give them their timeless value. Third, any great thinker's ideas rest back upon conceptions that he may take for granted, and often never directly states. It is what lies under the points that he makes that gives them lasting depth and abiding meaning. And it is these often unexpressed foundations of Paul's Gospel, which he takes for granted, that have in part given to his letters their feel of inspired worth.

This chapter has attempted to peel the orange ready for eating. Here Paul's letters have been set in order and laid open. It is possible now to taste their meat. For only as this background, with its far-reaching implications, is exposed and appreciated can one bite in and enjoy the juice of Paul's writings. It is this massive, often undisclosed background that gives to Paul's letters their profound, eternal value, and has caused them to be seized upon as inspired scripture. To that massive background we must now give our attention.

Chapter 7

THE CHRISTIAN THINKER

HIS MENTAL BACKGROUND

"Now I know in part."

THE MIND of every thoughtful person is enriched with a large background of ideas. These concern the whole scheme of the universe: this global earth, the vast interstellar spaces, and the long evolution of human society. But these basic conceptions the thoughtful person rarely puts on parade. Seldom does he discuss them formally. Others about him hold pretty much the same outlook. Explanation is not needed.

Paul, too, had his ideas of the entire created scheme of things. Because they were common knowledge in his day, he never expounded them systematically. Hence, one cannot find in any of his letters a chapter which can be labelled "Paul's Scheme of the Universe." But because the Gospel Paul proclaimed encompassed the entire creation, the whole history of man, and all the coming future, he could not avoid mentioning his background conceptions relative to how the universe is built. Since he was an evangelist, and not a professor of geography, astronomy or philosophy, he mentioned these things only incidentally. How he thought the universe was made and is operated can be found only by painstakingly weaving together his scattered references into a unified whole. This is difficult work, and requires solid thinking.

Paul lived in an ancient world, centuries before modern scientific instruments enabled men to explore the universe. Of necessity he held ideas at wide variance to those we automatically accept. Therefore, he is difficult to comprehend. It is never easy to enter another man's mind and see things as he sees them. It is thrice difficult for a modern mind to enter sympathetically into the mind of an ancient. But no full understanding of Paul's Gospel is possible without first knowing his scheme of the universe. To this we must now give our most active attention.

In Paul's universe, the Eternal World—Heaven—was above all, over all, and crowned all created things. Though Paul had many words to describe its quality, he never pictured its appearance. There were no pearly gates or golden streets in Paul's mind. He referred to this Eternal World as "things invisible." "Things invisible" cannot be pictured. They can be defined only as regards their quality. They were by nature "incorruptible." They were "incorruption"; that is, they could not be spoiled. They did not change; therefore the Eternal World was "abiding." It could neither alter nor pass away. Its central characteristic was "glory." This was Paul's chief word for the character of the Eternal World. By glory, Paul tried to suggest all the wonder, goodness and holiness we associate with the grace, power and self-giving love of God. The character of the Eternal World was glory: the glory of the character of God.

Below this glory world, in between it and the earth were the "heavens." They are not to be confused with Heaven. "The heavens," for Paul, were a vague region above the earth, but not exactly the same as Heaven. They were a part of the invisible world, beyond the reach of human eye. They were peopled with hosts of invisible spirits. Oddly enough to our thinking, these hosts of invisible spirits were chiefly malicious, forever bent upon human injury. Paul called them by a wide variety of names: "principalities," "powers," "rulers," "creatures" and "angels," the last meaning evil angels, or demons.

With them also were two malignant powers, "Sin" and "Death." We think of sin as moral wrongdoing—stealing, swearing, coveting, killing. So did Paul. Anyone doing these things would be a sinner. And we think of death as the cessation of bodily activity. So also did Paul. But for Paul Sin and Death were something more than moral wrongdoing and physical collapse. For him Sin and Death were living beings and, like the other malign spirits, were bent on disastrous human injury. Paul saw them as allied together for the one purpose of ruining men.

Back at the very beginning of Creation, Sin had made an assault on Adam by attacking him through his "flesh"—or physical body—and thus seizing possession of him. Through this seizure of Adam's flesh, Sin had been able ever since to enslave all Adam's descendants in the flesh. With Sin came Death, bringing man's final doom of both physical and moral destruction. So man became the helpless slave of Sin and the inevitable victim of Death. Here is how Paul puts it: "Therefore, as through one man [Adam] sin entered the world, and death through sin; and so death passed to all." In his Song of Immortality, Paul chants, "O death, where is thy sting? The sting of death is sin." Sin, this implies, is an evil force which, like some poisonous dragon, has stung man into moral paralysis, while Death stands ready to pounce upon him and carry him off.

All this is most puzzling to the modern mind. Sin for Paul is not merely wilful wrongdoing. It is a living power wreaking ruin upon men. Death is not only physical breakdown, but a live entity lying in wait for every man's life.

This means that Sin in its central aspects was beyond man's moral responsibility. It was more than the evil for which man is accountable. It was a cosmic power beyond his capacity to defeat. Strange as this seems to us, it was Paul's conception, and we need to understand it. For Paul, then, salvation was more than man's moral rehabilitation. Salvation required also that Sin and Death be fought and conquered. This was a part of the work of Christ. It was Christ's mission to encompass their defeat. As Paul puts it: "God, sending his own Son in the likeness of sinful flesh . . . condemned sin in the flesh." "For he [Christ] must reign, till he hath put all his enemies under his feet. The last enemy that shall be abolished is death."

This, then, was the Eternal World of Paul, invisible, incorruptible, and full of glory. It opened down into this Visible World of earth, sky and stars we so dearly know. This Visible World Paul never described. It lies about, under and over us. But again, as with the Eternal World, Paul described its character. It was in essence the full opposite of the World Above. It was "corruption," or "corruptible," something that was spoiled and spoiling. It was "decay" and "decaying." It "passeth away," forever changing, forever doomed to disappear. It was "subjected to vanity," and to "wrath," there being nothing solid or stable about it. And it "waiteth for the revealing of the sons of God . . . in hope that the creation itself also shall be delivered from the bondage of corruption into the liberty of the glory of the children of God."

Such was the physical universe of Paul. Morally it was a scene of sin-ridden desolation. Its only hope was that, along with the redemption of the children of Adam into the sons of God, it also would share in the great redemption.

Again the modern mind is bewildered. To speak of the

physical universe in religious terms of awaiting redemption is troublesome indeed. To talk not only of the salvation of men, but also of the deliverance of the round earth is foreign to all our thinking. But that was Paul, and we must appreciate his outlook. Sin and Death were not merely the moral acts of men, but cosmic evil powers which had corrupted not only men, but also the earth and stars. They, too, were under the law of decay and doom. They, too, awaited the coming of redemption.

Within this Visible World was another world, the World of Human Society. We think of human society as a collection of individual persons. Actually "society" does not exist of itself. It is nothing more than a lot of people, whom, taken together, we call society. But all this was not so with Paul. Just as Sin and Death were living powers, so with Paul, Human Society had an existence of its own. It had a kind of vague being on its own account. Here Paul's logic is clear. Since Sin and Death had demoralized the physical universe, and since they had corrupted man, through man's bodily nature they had corrupted Human Society. This strange conception of society will be clearer if we compare this point of view with our own view of physical inheritance. Each new generation does not start its physical life anew, but is produced out of the physical being of the parent generation. Our physical life is a continuing unity down the long generations. Its weaknesses, diseases, and passions pass down the years. In some such way as this Paul thought of Human Society. It was a kind of abiding social body that passed its good and evil down the march of time. But Paul had hope. If "as in Adam all die" through contaminating all Human Society, then "so also in Christ shall all be made alive," and the Social Order thereby be redeemed.

Within this social world stood the Individual Person. Paul saw him as a trinity of "Flesh," "Soul" and "Inward Man." By flesh, Paul usually meant the physical body, the visible material elements of life. Sin and Death, as Paul believed, had captured Human Life by invading the flesh, and through it so corrupting Human Society that the flesh can be of no aid in our salvation. It may be only morally indifferent, or it may rise up in the dire "sins of the flesh." "For I know that . . . in my flesh, dwelleth no good thing."

A second part of the Individual Person was "the Soul." Yet "Soul" but inadequately translates the meaning of 'psyche.' It included, for Paul, one's whole self-conscious life, all the essential personality apart from the body, the total psychical man with all his impulses and emotions. Since through the flesh Sin and Death have blasted this psychical nature, salvation involves its rescue and transformation by the empowering spirit of God. Hence, "The God of peace himself sanctify you wholly; and may your . . . soul [psyche] . . . be preserved entire, without blame at the coming of our Lord Jesus Christ."

The third element of the Individual Person is the "Inward Man," which was of the "invisible" world. This comes closest to our conception of the soul and the inner spiritual life. "Wherefore we faint not; but though our outward man [of flesh] is decaying, yet our inward man [of the "incorruptible" "abiding" world above] is renewed day by day." "For this cause I bow my knees unto the Father . . . that ye may be strengthened with power through his Spirit in the inward man." Being held in the keeping of the Flesh and Soul, this Inward Man also was in bondage to Sin and Death, awaiting its redemption.

These three: Flesh, Soul and Inward Man, constituted

for Paul the Individual Person. This total threefold human being Paul often referred to as "the body." To us with our understanding of the body as our physical organism, this is quite misleading. By the body, Paul meant the whole person, what we would call 'the self,' or the personality. "I beseech you therefore . . . to present your bodies a living sacrifice." This sounds as though Paul were saying, 'Keep your physique clean,' or 'Be ready to suffer martyrdom.' But not at all. A more correct translation, as one will find it in many modern phrasings, would be "I beseech you therefore . . . to present yourselves, as a living sacrifice," or 'present your whole personality,' or 'dedicate all your faculties,' or 'consecrate all you are,' body, mind and spirit, "a living sacrifice, holy, acceptable to God, which is your spiritual service."

This, in outline, is the strange physical and moral universe of Paul. A diagram at the close of this chapter may assist in clarifying its peculiarities for the reader. To us Death is not a wicked spirit enslaving men, but a natural physical process. Likewise, we see Sin not as a malicious power, but as wrong moral choices. The physical universe is not a moral but a material order. Nature for us is neither sinful nor saintly but the ongoings of a regular procedure we call, for want of a better term, 'Law.' [1] Society is not a bodily substance abiding through all generations, but a varying collection of persons. And man is not sinful because some invisible demon attacked an unknown ancestor millennia ago, but because he himself persists in wrongdoing. So one may

[1] But are we right? In the Bible sin is never just our misuse of innate powers; it is a terrible objective, external force invading the personality and encompassing its ruin. Likewise in the Bible the physical universe is never merely a natural order. It is part and parcel, also, of the moral order. It is under the destructive power of sin, and awaits the liberating power of the Gospel.

think he can quickly dismiss Paul as a back number, and laugh him off.

Yet, beneath his strange conception of the universe, Paul's moral principles are those we all must face. The physical world is in some aspects out of order, at least where man's bungling handiwork has robbed and abused it. It is subject to the blight of human evil. Also, society is in a sense a continuing process. It does not start anew each generation. It has been corrupted by human evil, and that evil becomes the corrupting environment of the succeeding generation. Again, man himself does not with each fresh generation begin sinning anew. He comes into the world equipped with irresistible compulsions to wrongdoing. Worse, he inherits the evil which his forebears have generated. He finds in himself the legacy of wickedness, bred through the previous long generations. Though morally he is responsible for his personal sin alone, actually he is the victim of the sin of the human race from its very beginning.

Thus while in structure Paul's universe may seem to us strange, or even absurd, in moral outlook it is a true description of the sorry tragedy in which human life is fixed. It is no wonder that Paul referred to "this present evil world" and looked forward to the joys of the age to come.

As to God's way of dealing with this tragic universe, two [2] other matters lay as basic principles in Paul's mind. The first

[2] Many other presuppositions underlay Paul's thinking, as: (1) The flat earth and the seven-storied heaven which in a vision Paul had penetrated "even to the third heaven"; (2) the jargon of the Mystery Religions about "knowledge" and "wisdom" which floated in the social air like our "evolution" and "science"; (3) the promised Messiah, whom Paul saw realized in the Risen Jesus; (4) clothing the resurrected personality with a "spiritual body," "incorruptible" and "as pleaseth Him"; (5) the speedy return of the exalted Christ in visible form, when Paul and other Christians then living should be "caught up . . . to meet the Lord in the air."

concerned the Law. In our English versions the reader will find Paul mentioning the Law at least one hundred and twenty-five times. It lay as a cornerstone beneath all his religious thinking. By the Law Paul meant the whole revelation of God through Moses and the prophets, all that we now call the Old Testament. In addition, as a loyal Pharisee he would include its *meaning* and meticulous observance as given by the great rabbis. At its core were imbedded the ritual practices sternly required of every Jew—circumcision, sacrifices, Sabbath keeping, food taboos, separation from gentiles, no image-making, and the sacred festivals. Central also were the great moral demands as embodied in the Ten Commandments.

Such a Law, given by divine revelation, was to Paul as sacred as is the Gospel to Christians. Its precious Scrolls, which were its symbol, he revered with the awe that Christians give to the blood-stained Cross. For Paul, the Law was God-given, absolute, perfect and eternal. "So that the law is holy, and the commandment holy, and righteous, and good." It was also a profound unity. One could not choose part, and reject part; obey some and ignore the rest. The whole Law was all of a piece. To break part was to break all. "Cursed is every one who continueth not in all things that are written in the book of the law." Every jot and tittle was the holy will of God.

But now the Law had been superseded by the Gospel. Here was a dilemma. The Law was God-given in all its details, and eternal. But the Gospel had abolished it. How could something so holy be both divinely given and eternal, and yet be superseded and done away? This contradiction Paul never fully solved. Surrender his conviction of the Law's divine order and eternal purpose he could not. All his training forbade that. Demand, then, that the Law be kept in force, he could not. All his experience forbade that. Unite the Law and the Gospel, as some were trying to do, subordinating the Gospel to the Law, he could not. The Gospel, he knew, exceeded the Law. Finding no logical way out of the dilemma, Paul turned to a practical solution.

The Law, he believed, had had a purpose, and that purpose stood forever. Its divine intent was to lead men to repentance. "The law came in besides, that the trespass might abound." It defined sin. It made clear what wrongdoing is. It thereby enlightened the conscience. The result intended was to lead every soul to repentance: "The goodness of God leadeth thee to repentance." But more. The Law was "become our tutor" whose purpose was to oversee one, and lead one out beyond the Law "to bring us unto Christ." The ancient Greek guardian to whom Paul refers (called "schoolmaster" in our Authorized Translation) held a place somewhat like that of the governess or master in wealthy English homes. His business is to oversee the daily life of the growing child, and lead it out of childhood into the independence and capabilities of adulthood. "The law is become our tutor [guardian] to bring us unto Christ, that we might be justified by faith." Ideally, Paul saw the Law as the direct road to Christ.

But at its very heart, the Law had a fatal weakness. It could only define sin. It could not provide the moral power to keep one from sinning. "The law had said, Thou shalt not covet: but sin, finding occasion, wrought in me through the commandment all manner of coveting." To endue one with the moral energy not to sin was exactly "what the law could not do, in that it was weak through the flesh." So Paul was left divided within himself. Keep the Law he must. But keep the Law he could not. "For I delight in the law of God after the inward man: but I see a different law in my members, warring against the law of my mind, and bringing me into captivity under the law of sin." So Paul was torn between his impulses and the Law's imperious demands which he could not keep. In tortured spiritual agony he cried, "Wretched man that I am! who shall deliver me?"

Paul finally resolved his dilemma, as we shall see more fully in the next chapter, not by careful logic, but by moral insight. There existed a principle older than the Law, deeper than the Law, and entirely outside the Law, by which God had always saved men. Long before Moses was given the Law, God had accepted Abraham on the grounds of simple faith. "Abraham believed God, and it was reckoned unto him for righteousness." God approaches men not as a lawgiver and judge, with condemnation, but with his forgiving grace as a Father. This forgiving grace man receives by his response of faith. As a result he is inwardly transformed by the Spirit's power, becoming a new man in Christ. Thus by one leap Paul landed with both feet planted squarely in the center of the Gospel. In his own mind he had reconciled both the divine grandeur of the eternal Law and the glory of the Gospel.

For us this is mostly water over the dam. Be it so. But the extensive space it occupies in Paul's letters requires that it be thoroughly understood. Otherwise much of Paul's thinking remains unrevealed. But more. Under it lies a perennial problem: the conflict between religious practice with its standards, regulations and rules of conduct, and the *change of heart* required if one is to be empowered to live worthily as a child of God. Be Christian in daily conduct the believer must, but he can never be so, triumphantly, until he has by faith put on the Lord Jesus Christ.

The other principle of God's dealing with this tragic

universe with which Paul grapples is the relation of Jesus' sacrifice to sin's forgiveness.

It must be noted first that blood-sacrifice was a universally accepted principle of religion throughout the ancient world. It was equally axiomatic to Jew and gentile alike. It received classic statement in *Hebrews*. "Apart from shedding of blood there is no remission." No blood-sacrifice, no forgiveness. This was one of the critical problems with which the author of *Hebrews* had to grapple. Christians no more offered blood sacrifices. But always, it was believed, blood *must* be offered if forgiveness be secured. The writer of *Hebrews* solved the problem by claiming that Jesus' blood, offered on the Cross, was blood offered for forgiveness. Jesus being the Son of God, his blood was shed once for all. Any further need of blood-offering was forever unnecessary. Blood had been offered, and by that blood-offering forgiveness had come.

It will be asked, why did humans come to think that God would not forgive without first receiving a blood-offering? The answer seems to lie in part in the sinner's conscience. He realized that evil-doing required recompense. Sin was no light matter, to be laughed off. Man, himself, must do something, give something as evidence of his sincerity. Also, the human mind is slow to believe in God's gracious willingness to freely forgive. We forgive slowly, grudgingly, and often not at all. Hence we conclude that God also is reluctant to forgive. Some gift must be presented God to win his forgiveness. Only so can one receive remission of sins.

If one asks, Why was it that blood came to be the medium of exchange? the answer is: In the ancient world blood was believed to be the seat of life, and therefore it was precious life itself. In the human organism just where is life deposited? In the heart? the lungs? the liver? We know now that life works through the proper functioning of the whole body. But the ancient, having no adequate physiology, believed that in the blood life was seated. "For the life of all flesh is the blood thereof." Hence, sin being so terribly evil, nothing less than life itself could be offered in hope of forgiveness.

Concerning blood offered for remission of sins, the reader is likely to recall that, just as Paul came to see that the way of faith was older than the Law and had always superseded it, so others long before had learned that no blood-sacrifice was ever required to secure God's forgiveness. "Thou delightest not in sacrifice. . . . Thou hast no pleasure in burnt offering," declared the ancient psalmist. "The sacrifices of God are a broken spirit: a broken and a contrite heart, O God, thou wilt not despise." God forgives without other offering than a repentant spirit.

This was the open way of Jesus. To the paralytic he said, "Son, thy sins are forgiven." At once his opponents cried, 'Blasphemy!' "Who can forgive sins but . . . God?" And that meant going to the temple and offering a sacrifice. But here was a Man saying in effect that forgiveness could be had just by repenting. Jesus' opponents saw the whole Mosaic system about to come tumbling down. All true religion, they thought, was in danger of obliteration. But Jesus persisted, and healing the man, sent him on his way without benefit of sacrifice. For Jesus, God demanded no offering, no blood, no sacrifice. And more, the God of Jesus does not wait for the sinner to come dragging an offering, but he, himself, sets out seeking the sinner, that he may find him, win him to repentance, and remit his sins. He indeed seeks and saves that which is lost!

But the idea of forgiveness by blood-sacrifice only was too

deeply rooted for the ancient world quickly to surrender. As Paul, enthralled by the Divine Grace, clung to the eternal glory of the Law, so, too, he seems to have kept something of his belief in blood-sacrifice. But it must always be remembered that in so doing he never got it down to the low level so often credited to him, of a 'financial' transaction whereby Jesus' blood is supposed to buy redemption.

Exactly how Paul thought of Jesus' blood as related to forgiveness is not clear. The sufferings of Jesus he mentions repeatedly. The blood of Jesus he names less than a half-dozen times. "Being justified freely by his grace through the redemption that is in Christ Jesus: whom God set forth to be a propitiation, through faith, in his blood." And again, "being now justified by his blood, shall we be saved from the wrath of God through him." And Paul speaks of Jesus as "having made peace through the blood of his cross." How this shedding of blood by Jesus gained forgiveness, Paul never explained. That he did not hold it as the crude ransom or substitutionary theory is certain. One thing he did see clearly which is forever true. He saw in Jesus' death a revelation, not of God's reluctance to forgive unless the sinner offered some token payment first, *but quite the opposite*. He saw in Jesus' sufferings the sure proof of God's eagerness freely to forgive on the ground of simple faith. For Paul, Jesus' bleeding death was God's revelation and evidence of his radiant willingness to grant freely remission of sins to all that call upon him. "God was in Christ reconciling the world unto himself."

Paul was everlastingly right in putting Jesus' death upon the cross central in his Gospel. Supremely it did exactly what Paul said it did. It set forth God's free offer of forgiveness, and showed to man the open way to the Father's heart. In deed and in truth, "God was in Christ reconciling the world unto himself," thereby "having made peace through the blood of his cross."

This, then, is the strange, weird universe of Paul. In it "the whole creation groaneth and travaileth in pain together" and "waiteth for the revealing of the sons of God." "This present evil world" awaits its deliverance into the glory of the age to come. How shall this creation, now subject to vanity and wrath, and all mankind held enslaved by Sin and Death, be saved? The answer to this was Paul's glorious message as the Gospel Preacher.

PAUL'S SCHEME OF THE UNIVERSE

A DIAGRAM

Paul's theory of the universe cannot be pictured. It can only be diagrammed. Above all is the Eternal World—Heaven, "invisible," "abiding," "incorruptible," "full of glory."

Below it are the Heavens, also a part of the invisible world. In it are the evil spirits, angels (demons), powers, rulers, principalities, and Sin and Death.

Note that this heavenly world opens directly and fully into the World Below. This is our visible universe, "subject to vanity," "corruption," "decay" and "wrath."

Within this visible universe is Human Society. To Paul's mind it possessed an entity and existence on its own account. And within the Human Society is each individual, with his "flesh," "soul," and "inner man."

The two arrows indicate the direction of Paul's thought. Sin and Death had gotten into life by effecting an entrance into Adam's flesh, thereby taking possession of his soul and inner man. Having done this, Sin and Death were able to

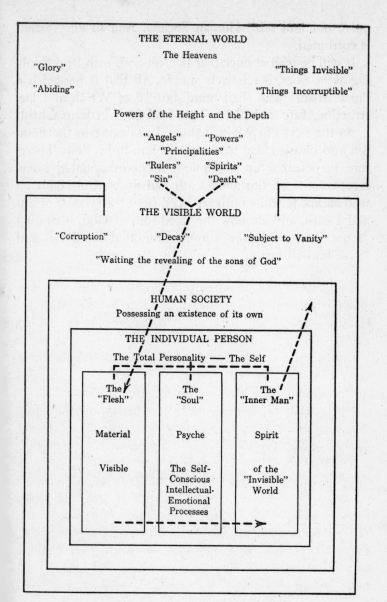

PAUL'S SCHEME OF THE UNIVERSE

move out and seize Human Society. And so all creation is corrupted.

It will be seen at once that the solution, with Paul thinking as he does, is relatively simple. All that is needed is a "new Adam" who shall bring, instead of Wrath and Destruction, Life and Light. This Paul finds in Jesus Christ.

As the next chapter will show, Jesus came in the flesh. Sin and Death failed to overpower him in his flesh. Therefore, he defeated Sin in the flesh. So he inaugurated a new race over which Sin and Death had no control. Thus all who accept Jesus by faith are freed from the tyranny of Sin and Death, and are now the freed sons of God, becoming "more than conquerors through him that loved us" and "gave himself for us."

Chapter 8

THE GOSPEL PREACHER

His Message

"I am not ashamed of the gospel."

PAUL POSSESSED a full, complete, systematic Gospel. It is often asserted that he never systematized his message. He spoke or wrote, it is charged, only for the immediate occasion. He had no call to work out his convictions in a thoroughly orderly fashion. It is true that he never expounded the background of his thought, as explained in the last chapter, in any explicit way. But Paul had his Gospel carefully systematized.

This Gospel he set forth in his letter to the Romans. Paul knew both in whom he believed and in what he believed. He had all the intricate interrelationships fully worked out. His was a vast, comprehensive system. It searched out the past unto its misty origins. It swept the present in every essential aspect. It penetrated the distant vistas of life eternal. It covered all the human mind can conceive of God, grasp of history, and understand concerning humanity. It was staggering in its significance. As I once heard a professor of philosophy assert, "The book of *Romans* is the most stupendous exhibition of intellectuality ever perpetrated upon the human intelligence." A thoroughgoing exposition of its details would require many large volumes. Yet, like all profound fathomings of life, Paul's

Gospel rests upon a handful of simple elements. Paul spoke and wrote to the most ordinary of people. His Gospel according to his letter to the Romans can be stated by answering a half-dozen simple questions.

What is the Gospel? (Chapter 1:16–17)

"It is the power of God unto salvation to everyone that believeth. . . . For therein is revealed a righteousness of God from faith unto faith." Each statement herein needs a brief explanation.

How do we know there is a Gospel? Because it is revealed to us. It is not a human invention. It is not a human discovery. Man by himself would never have guessed it. He had to be told. It is a revelation, a self-disclosure by God himself to men. It came from God to men. Later, Paul will add that this revelation is through Christ Jesus. What Jesus was, did and taught, is what is revealed. The point is that the Gospel is something *given* to us from God through Christ.

What is it that is revealed? Nothing less than the "righteousness of God." This righteousness is not merely that God does right and not wrong. It is not that God does justice and not injury. Nor is it that he expects good and not evil of men. All this is true. But with Paul the righteousness of God is something vastly more than moral rectitude. *It is his willingness to redeem sinful men.* God, looking upon man's stained and helpless condition, instead of despising and threatening him, is moved with compassion. Voluntarily God offers to rescue him. This offer "unto salvation" is God's "righteousness."

Just what is this salvation? In brief, it is man's total and eternal welfare. God is determined that everything that is best for man, everything that divine power can do for man both now and forever, shall be put at his disposal. A saved man has received "the power of God unto salvation." He has let God do for him all that God sees he needs. He has permitted God to make of him all that God sees is for him divinely possible. Later, Paul will be more explicit, declaring that all this is nothing less than becoming a "son of God," a personality with qualities and character like God's own righteousness.

Exactly whom is this salvation for? It is "unto everyone that believeth; to the Jew first, and also to the Greek." Sometimes Paul says it is unto the Greeks and the barbarians, or unto the wise and the foolish. In modern parlance, we might with honest accuracy rephrase it: Unto the Christian and the pagan, the cultured and boorish, the learned and ignorant. In brief, salvation is offered to *everyone without distinction.* God's righteousness is a universal offer. It is open to the best and the worst. All need it equally, the noblest and the meanest. Even the most unwilling are not despised. The offer is unremittingly pressed upon them. This righteousness of God in presenting salvation to men is content with nothing short of all mankind becoming the whole family of God.

How is this salvation to be obtained? "From faith unto faith." It is received by faith. It cannot be earned. It comes by a receptivity that sees God's offer, believes he will do what he has promised and, reaching out in spirit, takes it. "Faith" is accepting the offer of God's righteousness, that he is willing to save. In such bold acceptance of God's saving grace, human merit vanishes. God does it all. There is nothing left but to receive. It is as simple as though God said: 'Here, I have something wonderful for you,' and you, reaching forth and taking it, replied, 'Thanks, I've got it.' That, for Paul, is faith obtaining salvation. However, it must be noted that this receptivity requires in turn both appreciation and response. God's offer of salvation must be both valued and wanted. It is never forced. One must respond to it. One must see it, feel it, desire it, and "come and get it."

Finally, what does this salvation by faith do? It is "the power of God." Here is Paul's center and joy in the Gospel. It is not belief, though it involves convictions. It is not orthodoxy, though correct attitudes are implicit in it. It is not a code, though it works out into noble conduct. It is not ecclesiasticism, though it eventuates in the church. It is divine energy, moral change, spiritual transformation. Paul's pride in the Gospel sprang from what it does. The Gospel offers power to be changed, to live changed, and to change the face of society. "If any man is in Christ, he is a new creature." No wonder Paul cried, "I am not ashamed of the gospel!" "It is the power of God!"

Why do men need salvation? (Chapters 1:18–3:20)

"For all have sinned, and fall short of the glory of God." The "glory of God" is his divine likeness. When men have fallen short of the glory of God, they have failed to show forth this divine likeness which he expects of them. No man, anywhere, ever bore this divine likeness in its intended fulness. In one way or another frailty and Sin have obscured it. All men have fallen short. Hence, all men need salvation.

This hopeless plight of man Paul sees most convincingly manifested in religion. This one last power, that might rescue man when all others have failed, he has so perverted that it actually aids and increases his sinning. Paul sees man as a kind of immoral Midas. As everything Midas touched turned to gold, so everything man touches becomes corrupted with his sin. Man establishes democracy, but his

116

touch so infects it with partisanism, the spoils system and pressure groups, as to spell its doom. Man universalizes education, and then debauches it with propaganda, so that people, instead of being liberated by knowledge, become victimized by it. Man turns to religion, and then debases it into cold formalism so that instead of becoming the means of his salvation, it insures his condemnation.

This contagion Paul saw in both the natural religion of the pagan and the revealed religion of the Jew. The pagan had only a natural religion which he discovered by looking about and within him. "For God is manifest unto them . . . for the invisible things of him since the creation of the world are clearly seen, being perceived through the things that are made, even his everlasting power and divinity." The whole visible creation and the deep promptings of the soul Paul saw as natural, convincing evidences of God's presence, power, purity and goodness. Anyone should be able to read and understand them. But no. The pagans, though "knowing God, they glorified him not as God, neither gave thanks." And they went further and did worse. They did not give up belief in God and become atheists. They debased their conception of God. They "changed the glory of the incorruptible God for the likeness of an image of corruptible man." And they went further. They reduced God to the image "of birds, and four-footed beasts, and creeping things." So they got God down on all fours, crawling. They pointed to bulls, ibises, and snakes, and said, 'They represent God. God is like them.'

The result was an equally disastrous descent in morals. They gave themselves up "in the lusts of their hearts unto uncleanness," sexual perversions, and "being filled with all unrighteousness," manifested the putrid fruits of an evil spirit in "wickedness, covetousness, maliciousness, . . . envy, murder, strife, deceit, malignity," and became "insolent, haughty, boastful . . . disobedient, . . . covenant-breakers . . . unmerciful." And there Paul leaves them with a beast or insect for a god, and a code of immorals for morals. "Wherefore God gave them up." This is Paul's phrase for saying they were in complete spiritual and ethical bankruptcy. No possible seed of redemption lingered in them. Pagan society was morally rotting. It was devoid of all but a glimmer of moral vision. The very natural religion that should have been its great hope of rescue had become its final seal of total ruin. Only some power of God could save it.

As for the Jew, he was no better off. He did possess a better religion, given him by revelation. He had not discovered it for himself. It had been given him. It went beyond what natural religion could deduce from the universe about him. His was the religion of the Law. But like his pagan neighbor he had disobeyed and degraded it.

Paul, with all his admiration for the Law, saw that in spite of the Law's glory, the Jew was no better off than the gentile pagan. Through having the greater light of his revealed religion, the Jew condemned gentile belief and practice. Yet, says Paul, "Thou that judgest dost practice the same things." And because the Jew practiced the same things, he was under the same doom. "And reckonest thou this, O Man, who . . . doest the same, that thou shalt escape the judgment of God?" "For there is no respect of persons with God. As many as have sinned under the law shall be judged by the law." "But if thou bearest the name of a Jew, and restest upon the law, and gloriest in God, and knowest his will, and approvest the things that are excellent, being instructed out of the law, . . . teachest thou not thyself?" So the list of Jewish sins is similar to those committed by pagans—hypocrisy, stealing, adultery, and transgressions. The result among the gentiles, who had only their natural religion and should therefore have benefited by their proximity to Jews with their religion of revelation, was that "the name of God is blasphemed among the Gentiles because of you." The Law, which was meant to liberate men, had become the way of moral evasion, a source of snobbery over other peoples, and a system of petty ritualistic habits. The religion of light was made to deepen the darkness.

Thus the Jew, like the gentile, had turned the full circle. The revealed religion of the Law, so gloriously given to lead men to God, man had corrupted and twisted completely around. It now faced not the light but the dark. What had been revealed to him to ennoble him, he put to making himself the worse. The very glory of the Law he made to seal his doom. "Because by the works of the law shall no flesh be justified in his sight."

This, for Paul, is why men need salvation. All men have sinned and come short of the glory of God, and neither natural religion nor the revealed religion of the Law can save them. Worse, religion, the best gift of God, both natural and revealed, man has turned from the gift of salvation into a way of doom.

The end is "the wrath of God." "For the wrath of God is revealed from heaven against all ungodliness and unrighteousness of men." By wrath, Paul does not mean anger. Paul never uses anger in connection with God. He never thinks of God as 'getting mad.' Wrath is Paul's term for the natural consequence of breaking the moral law. Paul believed in a universe of a divinely enforced moral order. Just as we believe in a self-operating natural order, where if one breaks a law of nature he pays the consequences automatically; so Paul believed in a moral order where moral punishment follows with the same exact rigidity. "Whatsoever a man soweth, that shall he also reap." This sternly enforced moral law was for Paul "the wrath of God." Both pagans who despised their natural religion and turned it toward vice, and the Jews who debauched their revealed religion of the Law into sterile legalism have been left, so to speak, to 'stew in their own juice.' Like the broken laws of nature, the broken laws of morals pay off. All civilization is under "Wrath." Man is morally impotent, and terribly suffering.

Of course when Paul said "all have sinned, and fall short of the glory of God," he did not mean that there was not one decent pagan, or no godly Jews. There were many. But Paul saw the stark fact that man carries an inward depravity that blights his endeavors, stops his progress, and saps the power of religion to redeem him. The end is despair. He is "without hope." Only some new "power of God" can save him.

How, then, are men saved? (Chapters 3:21–4:25)

Salvation is provided by Christ on the condition of simple faith. "But now apart from the law a righteousness of God hath been manifested, being witnessed by the law and the prophets; even the righteousness of God through faith in Jesus Christ unto all them that believe; for there is no distinction; for all have sinned, and fall short of the glory of God; being justified freely by his grace through the redemption that is in Christ Jesus: whom God set forth to be a propitiation, through faith, in his blood, to show his righteousness. . . . that he might himself be just, and the justifier of him that hath faith in Jesus."

This long, complicated sentence merely rephrases Paul's

first statement of his Gospel. Again he says it is "revealed," being "manifested." Again it is the expression of the righteousness of God. Once more it is unto salvation, for by it men are justified. Once more it is unto everyone, for it is "unto all them that believe." And again it is received by faith, for it is unto those "that believe." And finally it operates as the power of God, in that it is "the justifier of him that hath faith in Jesus."

But to this repeated statement that the Gospel is the revelation of God's determination to save everyone by simple faith, Paul here adds two bedrock principles. First, this revelation of God's saving goodness comes through Jesus Christ. It presents salvation as "through the redemption that is in Christ Jesus: whom God set forth to be a propitiation, through faith, in his blood, to show his righteousness." It is because Jesus lived, suffered and rose again that we perceive God is willing to deal with sin on the only basis we can meet, namely, "faith." Jesus is God's declaration of his desire to forgive. The other added idea hides in the words, "propitiation" and "justify." These Paul connects with Jesus' blood. By propitiation he quite clearly suggests that Jesus' death is our means of knowing that God stands ready to forgive us. "Justify" is a now outmoded term meaning to 'make right,' 'declare innocent' or 'vindicate.' When a man is justified, he is vindicated. All charges against him are quashed. He goes forth exonerated. When, then, one accepts by faith God's offer of forgiveness, God justifies, or acquits him. He is declared innocent, forgiven. Boiled down this means: God has, through Jesus' death, shown us his eagerness to forgive all men who will come to him in simple faith. He will accept them when they so come, and from henceforth declare them guiltless.

Does all this sound terrifyingly complicated? There are

several reasons for this. First, our standard English versions are most awkwardly phrased. They obscure rather than clarify Paul's meaning. The reader will find modern speech translations far less complex and plainer. Next, Paul has here condensed his meaning. Condensed passages are usually difficult reading. So crowded together are Paul's ideas here that the great commentary by Sanday and Headlam, and that by C. H. Dodd require a dozen learned pages each to develop their implications. It takes Sanday and Headlam a full book-page in small newsprint type to clarify, just by paraphrase, this one brief passage.

A third reason these verses are so difficult is Paul's habit of speaking about God's forgiving grace in law court terms. The sinner is justified, acquitted, declared innocent. God is pictured as a judge. The sinner is haled into court as a law-breaker. But he cannot stand trial, for he knows he is guilty. Plead guilty he must, and throw himself on the mercy of the court. But instead of being sentenced, the Divine Judge declares him vindicated, acquitted, and he is set free. This is, of course, an extended figure of speech, a sort of parable. It must always be so understood and interpreted. It must never be taken literally. It will be noted at once that this is in strong contrast with Jesus. He never spoke of the sinner as standing before a judge as a culprit. He presented God as "your heavenly Father," and put forgiveness on the basis of family relationship. Hence his Gospel appears much simpler and more vital than Paul's. But Paul is not so far from Jesus as he seems. Under his figures of judge, convict, trial and acquittal is essentially the same Gospel. God in his grace offers men forgiveness freely like a father, "through faith."

The final reason why this passage is so troublesome is that Paul here deals with the profoundest problem with which the human mind can grapple—the forgiveness of sins. Here is God in the splendor of his holiness. Here is man in the helplessness of his sinfulness. What can be done? Man can be duly punished. But punishment of itself neither heals nor restores. It merely smites. Only forgiveness can save and redeem. But there is a false forgiveness that seems to make sin of no consequence. It says in effect, 'Sin doesn't matter.' But sin does matter! Look at the ruin it spreads! Behold the disintegration of soul it effects! Forgiveness must still show sin matters. Furthermore, how do we know a God of exacting righteousness and pure holiness will, or even can, forgive? Would he not thereby surrender his righteousness and holiness?

These queries haunt the minds of earnest thinkers when they consider the forgiveness of sin. Granted that they often spin out these problems into a tangled web of imaginary issues, these are honest questions. And for their solution Paul has true answers. Man's only hope lies in being forgiven. Jesus' death shows not only how willing God is to forgive, but also how serious both sin and forgiveness are. This grace of forgiveness, this "power of God," man may have on the only terms possible for him to meet, namely, by faith. He may have it freely and gladly by receiving the forgiveness of God through Christ Jesus.

Thus Paul re-states his Gospel. He then proceeds to show that this way of salvation by faith through Christ is the one way God has always dealt with men. "Abraham believed God, and it was reckoned unto him for righteousness." Salvation by faith is the old, historic method of God, "being witnessed by the law and the prophets." God has always saved men by faith alone. From the beginning with Abraham, whom God accepted by faith centuries before the Law was given to Moses, this way of faith has continued down the years. For Abraham "received the sign of circumcision, a seal of the righteousness of the faith which he had . . . that he might be the father of all them that believed . . . that righteousness might be reckoned unto them." Abraham's true children are any who accept God's gracious offer by faith. The final proof and seal that this really is God's only way with men is now revealed in the death of Jesus Christ. For it was written "for our sake also, unto whom it shall be reckoned, who believe on him that raised Jesus our Lord from the dead, who was delivered up for our trespasses, and was raised for our justification."

It is now clear that Paul conceives of his Gospel as the one profound principle operating in the spiritual universe. Just as gravitation in its ramifications is the profound power that holds the stellar universe together from its wide-ranging, outmost star to its smallest particle of dust, and just as it is a continuous force from the dawn of the first vague nebulae, so Paul sees that salvation by faith, freely offered to men, is God's only method of dealing with men. It is as old as man, as wide-reaching as all peoples, and endureth through all generations. It is the one foundation of the moral universe.

By this universality Paul's Gospel outreaches the natural religion of the pagans. It includes more than man can discover by exploring the starry heavens above, or learn by minutely examining his soul within. Also it stretches out beyond all bounds of the Law, which for most Jews meant a series of stringent regulations to be strictly obeyed. No man, Jew or gentile, could by himself invent a fatherly God, dream up Jesus Christ, or devise forgiveness by faith alone. Thus Paul's Gospel added something new. It proclaimed the living power of God through the personality of Jesus Christ, offering to all men by faith the joy and peace of pardon. Occasionally rare souls had realized this amazing Gospel: the author of the Fifty-first Psalm with "Thou delightest not in sacrifice; else would I give it. . . . A broken and a contrite heart, O God, thou wilt not despise," and the writer of *Isaiah* 55: "Seek ye Jehovah . . . let the wicked forsake his way" and "he will abundantly pardon." Now Paul sees it verified in Christ. The sole condition is faith. Faith is the one condition all men can meet. Anyone can receive. It presents no barrier of belief, race or ritual. Whosoever will may accept this Father-God as revealed by the dying Jesus. By faith alone he is freely pardoned. And being so forgiven, the receiver now stands ready to obtain the rich benefits of salvation.

What are the benefits of salvation? (Chapters 5–8)

They are the blessings that come with a new life in the Spirit, and a new character. "Being therefore justified by faith, we have peace with God through our Lord Jesus Christ; through whom also we have had access by faith into this grace wherein we stand; and we rejoice in hope of the glory of God." In Christ, then, the believer by faith comes into a new life.

The nature of this new life Paul proceeds to describe. He says it brings the assurance of "glory." Glory, as we have seen, is Paul's way of describing the splendor which characterizes the essential nature of the heavenly world. When the believer receives salvation by faith, there blossoms in him the very glory world itself. All that it is, he now becomes! Here and now he is lifted out of his life in the flesh, though he still lives in the flesh. He possesses the qualities that belong to the glory. His is the glory and incorruption of the heavenly splendor.

At once the believer is freed from the power of Death.

Of course he will die physically. But to Paul, as we saw, Death is a quasi-being whose malignant power destroys both body and soul. But now, having received salvation by faith, he is lifted to a new level of life Death cannot reach. The incorruption and glory in him are immune to Death. "Death no more hath dominion over him." Moreover, the believer is freed from the slavery of Sin. Sin Paul also conceives as a semi-being which holds all mankind in bondage. Now the believer's new life of glory liberates him from slavery to Sin. The life in Christ, Sin has no power to shackle. Paul does not say that the believer cannot, or will not, ever sin. But he does suggest that he need not sin. "Our old man [ourselves before accepting salvation by faith] was crucified with him [Christ], that the body of sin might be done away, that so we should no longer be in bondage to sin. . . . For sin shall not have dominion over you." "But now being made free from sin and become servants to God, ye have your fruit unto sanctification, and the end eternal life." The thrall of Sin is broken.

The glorious result is that the believer knows himself now as a Son of God. He has had a new birth. He has a new Parent. He is become a new person. "For as many as are led by the Spirit of God, these are sons of God . . . whereby we cry, Abba, Father. The Spirit himself beareth witness with our spirit, that we are children of God."

This becoming a new person in Christ is one of Paul's central convictions. When a man receives Christ, he becomes in effect *somebody else.* "If any man is in Christ he is a new creature." He becomes a member of a new species. He was a human being. Now he is a heavenly person. He was born of woman. Now he is born of God. He did belong to the Kingdom of Earth. Now he is joined to the Kingdom of Heaven. He had possessed the qualities, habits, instincts and reactions of human passions: "fornication, uncleanness, ... idolatry, sorcery, ... strife, jealousies, ... drunkenness, revellings, and such like." But now as a man born, as John put it, "not of blood, nor of the will of the flesh, nor of the will of man, but of God," he is a heavenly being whose qualities of spirit are those of glory. He now possesses a new set of instincts and reactions. He now manifests not the acts of the flesh, but the fruits of the Spirit: "Love, joy, peace, long suffering, kindness, goodness, faithfulness, meekness, self-control." The believer is indeed a son of God.

This passing over from life in the flesh to life in the Spirit, from the Sin-enslaved earthly life of corruption to the Spirit-freed heavenly life of glory, Paul describes with four illustrations. His first carries out the contrast between Adam and Christ. "For as in Adam all die, so also in Christ shall all be made alive." It is built upon Paul's peculiar conception of the universe, as explained in the preceding chapter, and in the diagram at this chapter's close. If through Adam all men could be infected to their ruin by Sin and Death, so through Christ, whosoever receives him by faith can be endued with divine life. "For if by the trespass of the one [Adam] the many died, much more did the grace of God, and the gift by the grace of the one man, Jesus Christ, abound unto the many. ... For if, by the trespass of the one [Adam], death reigned through the one [Adam]; much more shall they that receive the abundance of grace and of the gift of righteousness reign in life through the one, even Jesus Christ." As one inherited the disaster of Sin in the flesh, so on becoming a son of God, one inherits the glory life of Christ.

For his next illustration Paul turns to the Christian ritual of baptism. He allegorizes it into terms of Jesus' death and resurrection. The convert's immersion he calls a dying. The believer's evil nature is, as it were, drowned. More, this figurative dying, Paul, as in a parable, links with Christ's dying. The believer's immersion is a sort of going down into the grave with Christ. Then the convert comes up out of the water. This Paul calls his resurrection to a new life. He is "risen with Christ." Just as Jesus went into the tomb as a slain person, but rose the Lord of Glory, so the convert goes down into the water as a child of the flesh, but rises out of the water a child of glory. "Or are ye ignorant that all we who were baptized into Christ Jesus were baptized into his death? We were buried therefore with him through baptism into death: that like as Christ was raised from the dead through the glory of the Father, so we also might walk in newness of life. For if we have become united with him in the likeness of his death, we shall be also in the likeness of his resurrection." As Christ died to this earth, and rose again to the new life of eternity, so the believer dies to the old life of the flesh and rises to the new life in the Spirit.

For his third illustration Paul turns to the institution of slavery. The believer before receiving salvation by faith, Paul now represents as enslaved by Sin. He was not his own. He was in chains to Evil. But now he is liberated to a freedom which becomes in turn a willing slavery to righteousness. "But thanks be to God, that, whereas ye were servants of sin, ye became obedient . . . and being made free from sin and servants to God, ye have your fruit unto sanctification." Emancipated from Sin, the believer is now at liberty to live as a free son of God.

Finally, Paul turns to the institution of marriage. Just as a wife or husband is freed in case of a partner's death from the marriage bond, so the believer having accepted salvation by faith is now free from the bond of Sin and Death. "For the woman that hath a husband is bound by law to the husband while he liveth; but if the husband die, she is discharged from the law of the husband. . . . Wherefore, my brethren, ye also were made dead to the law through the body of Christ; that ye should be joined to another, even to him who was raised from the dead, that we might bring forth fruit unto God." Sin and Death no longer have any claim. The believer is now free to begin his new life in Christ.

These illustrations will seem to many flat and artificial. It will help if we see them for what they are, illustrations. They are not theological arguments. They must not be used as stones in a theological system. They afford no light on the nature of the physical universe, the proper method and meaning of baptism, and exact analysis of sin and death, nor rules regulating marriage and divorce. They are four illustrations meant to illumine one fact, the new life hid with Christ in God. They attempt to set forth the certainty, wonder and holiness of the new, incorruptible, glory life, as contrasted with the old natural life. A new life whose quality is glory, whose power is victory over all sin, whose future is freed from the threat of death, whose nature is to produce the fruits of the Spirit, and whose joy is peace and gratitude as a son of God! That is Paul's abiding meaning here.

So glorious is this becoming a "new creature" in Christ that Paul becomes ecstatic. He, who was once "breathing threatening and slaughter against the disciples of the Lord," as a hard, cruel, vindictive man, had himself become a new person in Christ. Now he could write about love that "suffereth long, and is kind," and "Love never faileth." He knew himself to be literally somebody else. Once he had been morally impotent, doing "what I would not." Now he knew himself as a son of God, free, radiant, victorious.

Ecstatically he unfolds the glory of his life in the Spirit. It removes all sense of guilt. "There is therefore now no condemnation to them that are in Christ Jesus." It lifts one to a heavenly level of action. Henceforth the believer walks "not after the flesh, but after the Spirit." God no longer is conceived as judge or taskmaster, but as the heavenly Father, "whereby we cry, Abba, Father." One sees himself as one of the "children of God: and if children, then heirs; heirs of God, and joint-heirs with Christ." Suffering now becomes a very small thing, "not worthy to be compared with the glory that shall be revealed to us-ward." Even nature shall share in the glorious redemption. "The creation itself also shall be delivered from the bondage of corruption into the liberty of the glory of the children of God." Prayer becomes the very Spirit of God praying within us to the God above us. "The Spirit also helpeth our infirmity" and "maketh intercession for us . . . according to the will of God." Finally, even the agonies of this life are also redeemed by the grace of God. For God 'cooperates in all things for good.'

This contemplation of the glory of being "in Christ," Paul is no longer able to expound, explain or illustrate. He can only sing. And he bursts into a hymn of Victory:

> What then shall we say to these things?
> If God is for us, who is against us?
> He that spared not his own Son,
> But delivered him up for us all,
> How shall he not also with him
> Freely give us all things?
>
> Who shall lay anything
> To the charge of God's elect?

130

It is God that justifieth;
Who is he that condemneth?
It is Christ Jesus that died,
Yea rather, that was raised from the dead,
Who is at the right hand of God,
Who also maketh intercession for us.

Who shall separate us from the love of Christ?
Shall tribulation, or anguish, or persecution,
Or famine, or nakedness, or peril, or sword? . . .
Nay, in all these things we are more than conquerors
Through him that loved us.

For I am persuaded,
That neither death, nor life,
Nor angels, nor principalities,
Nor things present, nor things to come,
Nor powers, nor height, nor depth,
Nor any other creature,
Shall be able to separate us from the love of God,
Which is in Christ Jesus our Lord.

But what of those who refuse this gospel? (Chapters 9–11)

Here Paul discusses the problem as it is related to the unconverted Jews only. For him the Christians, Jewish and Gentile, were already saved. So would be the gentiles who, while not yet converts, were fast crowding in. Paul apparently did not envision any gentiles as finally and forever refusing the Gospel. Having started to come in, he seems to have expected them all to enter. There remained only the unconverted Jews to be considered. What of these Chosen People, keepers of the Law, who had refused the New Covenant? It is not necessary here to trace Paul's rather involved and somewhat unsatisfactory argument. His conclusion is that eventually "all Israel shall be saved."

Everything depends upon the absolute sovereignty of

God. "For he saith to Moses, I will have mercy on whom I have mercy. . . . So then it is not of him that willeth, . . . but of God that hath mercy. . . . O man, who art thou that repliest against God? Shall the thing formed say to him that formed it, why didst thou make me thus? . . . What if God, willing to show his wrath, and to make his power known, endured with much longsuffering vessels of wrath fitted unto destruction: and that he might make known the riches of his glory upon vessels of mercy, which he afore prepared unto glory?" Here is what at first appears to be the Eternal Sovereignty in its most extreme and arbitrary form. It seems to say: God is the great and awful Absolute. None dare question by a whisper his almighty will. He refuses whom he refuses, and saves whom he saves. None dare query him or say him nay.

This is quite revolting to the modern mind. About it certain comments need to be made. First, Paul is basically right. The universe is not in its origin and construction democratic. We do not vote on how we will have it! Object to it as we may please, there is not a thing we can do. In this matter God is sovereign and forever unreachable. As Job saw long before Paul, no man can say to God, "What doest thou?" Or as Paul puts it here, no man can say to him, "Why didst thou make me thus?" Nor can we summon God to explain his mercy toward men. He offers it on his own terms. "I will have mercy on whom I will have mercy. . . . So then he hath mercy on whom he will." We did not invent the goodness of God. Of his own accord he freely offers us his grace. We can but accept or reject. God is forever sovereign.

The second fact to note is that Paul here asserts the Absolute Sovereignty of God is directed toward the salvation of men. God, for Paul, is a moral being. Having made things as they are, beholding man as he is, he assumes sole responsibility for all things. He has voluntarily taken upon himself the burden of rescuing man. For Paul the divine sovereignty has but one purpose, the salvation of men, "that he might have mercy upon all."

Nor can this sovereignty be finally defeated. If so, God would not be sovereign. His whole order might then be overthrown and another prove himself to be God. For Paul, this was totally inconceivable. God will be finally victorious.

Unfortunately, Paul's argument is neither logical nor complete. While he seems to insist on the final salvation of his Jewish brethren, he also insists that God "hath mercy on whom he will, and whom he will he hardeneth." Paul ignores the problem of previous generations of both Jews and gentiles who were compelled to live without the Gospel. He passes by his previous declaration that men are judged according to the light they possess and heed. Nor does he face the possibility that both Jews and gentiles will continue rejecting the Christ.

Thus Paul's logic here is confused and inconclusive. But his conviction is written clear. Ultimately the Divine Sovereignty will be triumphant. The Divine Sovereignty is at heart sacrificial grace expending itself in rescuing men. "For Christ is the end of the law unto righteousness to everyone that believeth." For Paul there could follow but one sure result. Such power and grace can never be permanently rejected. Eventually "all Israel shall be saved."

Again Paul is filled with awe and wonder. Again, contemplating the goodness and power of God, he bursts into a hymn of adoration:

> O the depth of the riches
> Both of the wisdom
> And the knowledge of God!
> How unsearchable are his judgments,
> And his ways past tracing out!

For who hath known the mind of the Lord?
Or who hath been his counsellor?
Or who hath first given to him,
And it shall be recompensed unto him again?

For of him, and through him,
And unto him, are all things.
To him be the glory forever.
Amen.

Finally, *what shall be the daily life of those saved by faith?* (Chapters 12–15)

It is to be a life consecrated to God which expends itself in humble brotherly service. For Paul, the Gospel meant a new order of daily living. Men who had become "new creatures" and "sons of God" were to manifest it in a higher plane of action. Every phase of life's day-by-day relationships was to be transformed, even transfigured, upon the heavenly level.

First, the believer must yield himself to God in glad consecration. "I beseech you therefore, brethren, by the mercies of God, to present [yourselves] a living sacrifice, holy, acceptable to God. . . . And be not fashioned according to this world: but be ye transformed by the renewing of your mind, that ye may prove what is the good and acceptable and perfect will of God."

Second, let the believer humbly acknowledge his limitations. "For I say . . . to every man that is among you, not to think of himself more highly than he ought to think; but so to think as to think soberly, according as God hath dealt to each man a measure of faith."

Next, he must acknowledge his constant need of the brotherhood of his fellow followers of Christ. They have need of him, but even more, he has need of them. "We, who are many, are one body in Christ, and severally members, one of another."

Again, he must flame with an all-sided, incandescent, active love. He must sacrifice himself on behalf of the varied needs of his fellow Christians. "Let love be without hypocrisy. . . . In love of the brethren be tenderly affectioned one to another. . . . Avenge not yourselves, . . . overcome evil with good."

Furthermore, he must be a good citizen. Laws pertaining to the social good are to be scrupulously obeyed. Sovereign power on earth derives from the sovereign power of God. In so far as it honors his glory, honoring it honors God. Disregarding it disregards him. "Let every soul be in subjection to the higher powers: for there is no power but of God. . . . Therefore he that resisteth the power, withstandeth the ordinance of God."

Sixth, he must be sure to fulfill all debts and obligations of whatever nature. His only undischargeable debt should be the perpetual duty to love. "Render to all their dues: tribute to whom tribute is due; custom to whom custom; fear to whom fear; honor to whom honor. Owe no man anything, save to love one another."

Finally, he must exercise kindly toleration to all in matters of disputed conscience. If others have seemingly narrow scruples on minor matters that are debatable, do not offend them. "Let us not therefore judge one another any more: but judge ye this rather, that no man put a stumbling block in his brother's way, or an occasion of falling." "Now we that are strong ought to bear the infirmities of the weak, and not to please ourselves."

"Now the God of peace be with you all. Amen."

The question remains: How far is this carefully systematized scheme of salvation as proclaimed by Paul true? Does it represent the facts of God's grace as it really works? At once a distinction should be made between Paul's Gospel and the framework in which he places it. There is, of course, no permanent validity in Paul's conception of the structure of the universe, the quasi-personality of Sin and Death, and the metaphysical solidarity of human flesh down the generations. These are no abiding part of his exposition of God's saving grace. They form only the framework for Paul's scheme. They are a kind of first-century-period mental furniture, of a style long outmoded.

But Paul's Gospel itself says: Man is incurably sinful. Only God's power as revealed in Christ is sufficient to save him and re-create him a child of God. Is this forever true? The glorious answer is, *any man can prove it for himself.* He need take no man's word for it. He need rest his conviction on no elaborated proofs. He can have it demonstrated in his own soul.

As to man's helpless moral condition, one has only to look about. In the recesses of one's own heart, in the structure of society, in the processes of government, in the practices of commercial enterprise—all are blighted by the curse of evil. Political chicanery, class rivalries, economic injustices, racial enmities, religious divisions, national jealousies, global hostilities and individual moral collapse cry aloud, "All have sinned, and fall short of the glory of God."

But, then, does this saving power of God come through Jesus Christ? Again, a man may prove it for himself. It was this letter to the Romans that brought moral repentance to Augustine, spiritual light to Luther, peace of soul to Wesley, preaching power to Barth, and is now rescuing modern theology from its impotent proclamation of salvation by inevitable, gradual, painless progress. For these twenty centuries Paul's Gospel has been doing mighty business. But one does not need to confine his investigations to the examples of history. He may try out this Gospel in his own soul. He may acknowledge his moral impotence, surrender himself to the glory of God in Christ, be re-created to a new life in the Spirit, and know in his own heart how "The Spirit himself beareth witness with our spirit, that we are the children of God!"

Stripped, thus, of its first-century raiment, Paul's Gospel stands forth in radiant simplicity. The whole saving truth of God is encompassed by six basic questions! Imagine a scene in some slum mission. Wretched derelicts stagger in, seeking light and warmth. One of the speakers, himself a recently converted down-and-outer, might effectively present his message by the use of Paul's six points:

The big power of God is ready to save you guys.

You are suffering for your sins, and haven't got the strength to quit.

But you can get saved by giving yourselves to Jesus, who died that you might be cleaned up.

If you'll accept what God can do for you, He will clean you up, and give you strength to live decent.

Of course you can refuse, like you've been doing. But if you ever get decent again, it can be only by accepting Jesus and letting Him put you on your feet.

And when you've got saved, you'll be able to quit bumming, be trustworthy and live respectable.

Crude? Yes. Bad grammar? Certainly. But it embodies the gist of *Romans*. It sets forth the essence of Paul's Gospel!

This is the genius of Paul's Gospel, and the glory of salvation by faith through Christ Jesus. Its essential message is so elemental and vital that it can be stated in the half-literate terms of the gutter, yet rich enough to be clothed in the classic phrases of the profoundest theology.

This Gospel offers the salvation of God to everyone who will accept it by faith. For all men are enslaved in Sin and possess no power to liberate themselves. For them God has provided salvation through Christ on the condition of simple faith. This salvation brings the believer a new life and character, and victory over all evil through the power of the indwelling Spirit. Eventually all men must yield to its irresistible power. Whoever has received this salvation by faith must show his gratitude for this free grace of God by a consecrated life, brotherly love, good citizenship, and kindly toleration.

Different though this Gospel of Paul appears, it is basically Jesus' Gospel as depicted in the parable of the Prodigal Son. There is the wilful boy bent on evil and headed for destruction. There is sinful society lying in wait to compound evil with evil to enlarge and complete his ruin. There he stands among the swine in ragged want, without power to better himself. There is his good father eager, hoping, waiting, seeking. There is the repentant boy welcomed back to his father's house with joy, given all things needful, given added things beautiful, and restored to sonship. With all its Jewish and Hellenic embellishments, *Romans* at its heart proclaims the Gospel of Jesus!

PAUL'S SCHEME OF SALVATION

The Diagram [1]

Over all is the Eternal World, invisible, incorruptible, abiding and full of glory.

In it, in the heavens above the earth, exist the evil powers, angels (demons), rulers, Sin and Death.

Then God created Adam. Sin and Death seized upon Adam through his flesh. Thus at the start all future humanity was polluted and ruined. "For since by man [Adam] came death," "For as in Adam all die," "The first man [Adam] is of the earth, earthy," "As is the earthy, such are they also that are earthy," "Through one man [Adam] sin entered into the world, and death through sin; and so death passed unto all men, for that all sinned."

After Adam, Paul conceived the human race as dividing into two great halves. One part is, of course, his own people, the Jews. These he sometimes called the Chosen People, or Israelites. The other half composed all the non-Jewish world, the gentiles.

Each of these halves Paul sees as again split in two. Of the two groups of Jews, one part is Unfaithful Israel, who has not kept the covenant nor responded to the gospel of Christ. The other part is the Faithful Jews, called by the prophets "The Remnant." These were obedient to the Law, and they accepted the Gospel as the fulfillment of the covenant. Together these two groups constitute "All Israel."

In the similarly divided gentile world, Paul sees one

---

[1] The reader should try to see this diagram as if it were superimposed over the one in the previous chapter, so that Human Society with the Individual Person as "Flesh," "Spirit" and "Inner Man" merges into this diagram to form a complete design of Paul's world.

group as those gentiles who have responded to the Gospel message. The other group are those who have not yet done so. Together these two gentile halves make up "the full number of the Gentiles."

Down the centuries the divisions continued. Mankind was under the thraldom of Sin and Death. After the long march of the centuries Jesus came: "God sending his own son in the likeness of sinful flesh and for sin, condemned sin in the flesh."

Jesus came. He belonged to our flesh, being "of the seed of Abraham." But he was a New Adam, or Second Adam, in whom began a new race or "new creation." What happened, according to Paul, was that Jesus, being in the flesh, Sin and Death immediately tried to get possession of him through his flesh, as they had done with Adam. But in the flesh Jesus fought Sin and Death and defeated them. He was not polluted. So, just as Adam's descendants are polluted because Sin and Death polluted him, Jesus' descendants by faith could not be corrupted, as Sin and Death could not corrupt him. Therefore anyone who accepted Christ by faith entered a new inheritance. He no longer inherited Adam's pollution from Sin and Death. He inherited Christ's Light and Life. "So then as through one trespass [Adam's] the judgment came unto all men to condemnation; even so through one act of righteousness [Jesus' victory over Sin and Death] the free gift came unto all men to justification of life. For as through the one man's disobedience [Adam's] the many [all mankind] were made sinners, even so through the obedience of the one [Christ] shall the many [all mankind] be made righteous." "For since by man [Adam] came death, by man [Christ] came also the resurrection of the dead. For as in Adam all die, so also in Christ shall all be made alive."

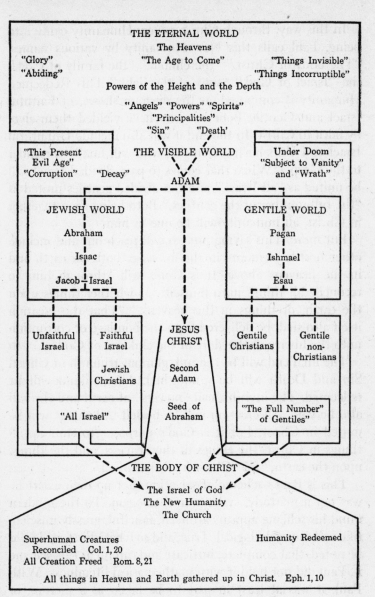

PAUL'S SCHEME OF SALVATION [2]

[2] Adapted from C. H. Dodd, *Romans,* Moffatt New Testament Commentary, p. 187, Harper & Bros., New York, by permission.

In this way, through Christ a New Humanity came into being. Paul calls this New Humanity by various names, "The body of Christ," "the church," "the family of God," the "Israel of God," "sons of the light." This Redeemed Humanity is composed, as the diagram shows, of Faithful Israel and Gentile Believers who have yielded themselves by faith to Christ. In the end it will also include Unfaithful Israel and Unbelieving Gentiles, who will finally surrender to the Gospel. When that comes to pass, divided Israel will be united as "all Israel," and the divided gentiles united as "the full number of the gentiles." Both being then together in Christ, all humanity will be one in him.

But more. This saving process will reach out and include other hostile elements in the universe, both on earth and in the heavens above. It is God's will "through him to reconcile all things unto himself . . . whether things upon the earth, or things in the heavens." "That the creation itself also shall be delivered from the bondage of corruption unto the liberty of the glory of the children of God."

The final end will be the full, glorious triumph of Christ. Sin and Death will be vanquished. All mankind will be redeemed. The invisible evil "powers" of earth and sky will also be won. All creation will be healed. All things will be united in Christ. For it is God's purpose "to sum up all things in Christ, the things in the heavens, and the things upon the earth," for "Christ is all, and in all."

This is Paul's scheme of salvation. Let no man assert he was not a masterly, systematic theologian. To the modern mind his scheme appears artificial, fanciful, grossly unscientific and unpsychological. True, and so what? First, it should be noted, that complete, intricate and careful as this scheme is, Paul did not hold it with mathematical literalness. With Paul, it was at least in part to be taken as a picture, or parable of man's condition, Christ's work, and history's hope. For in *Romans* 5:14 he says that Adam "is a *figure* of him [Christ] that was to come." This scheme, Paul realized, could not encompass the glory of God in Christ, which outreaches all possibility of precise statement. He is compelled to fall back on figurative language. Adam is the "figure," the "foreshadowing," the "type," the "pre-figuring" of all Christ was and has done for men.

But what abides here is plain. Mankind is thoroughly and universally corrupted and prone to sin. In his natural state he is morally helpless. Evil is more than a failure of will. It is a force that affects the creation at large. But the appearance of Christ changed everything. By faith in him, God was reconciling the world unto himself, re-creating man as a New Humanity, the sons of God; restoring the whole created order, and exalting Christ to the throne of the universe, where he shall reign over all and in all.

Chapter 9

THE TRIUMPHANT MARTYR

The Disputed Closing Years

"I am already being offered."

THE CLOSING YEARS of Paul's life after his arrival under arrest in Rome are, unfortunately, in dispute. Except for a bit of tradition and references in the Prison epistles of *Philippians, Colossians* and *Philemon,* and the *Pastoral* letters of I and II *Timothy* and *Titus* all is silence.

Taking these letters, as was heretofore commonly done, at their face value, and as written from Rome, one could piece out a neat story. *The Acts* left Paul as a prisoner under detention in Rome. But he had freedom to live where he would, receive such friends as he pleased, and preach his Gospel unmolested. "And he abode two whole years in his own hired dwelling, and received all that went in unto him, preaching the kingdom of God, and teaching the things concerning the Lord Jesus Christ with all boldness, none forbidding."

Then what happened? The older view saw Paul released, making his long-planned journey to Spain, and also another swing about the Aegean basin, again visiting his beloved churches. Then he was rearrested, taken to Rome, tried, condemned and executed. For the Prison epistles picture Paul as successfully evangelizing "Caesar's household" and "the whole praetorian guard." They also picture him as planning to revisit his Aegean churches, and say that he intended to "send Timothy shortly unto you," and "I myself also shall come shortly." He even asked that Philemon at Colossae should "prepare me also a lodging."

The long-hoped-for trip to Spain is attested by early though vague tradition. Clement of Rome, writing about 95 A.D., or only some thirty years after Paul's death, says, "Paul played the herald in the east and the west, having taught the whole world righteousness, and passed to the boundaries of the west." The *Muratorian Fragment*, an early Christian writing dating about 170 A.D., adds, "Luke [in *The Acts*] omitted . . . Paul's journey to Spain."

His journey back among his Aegean churches may be vaguely traced from references in the Pastoral epistles. In *Titus* Paul mentions being in Crete. In I and II *Timothy* he mentions being in Miletus, Ephesus, Troas, Macedonia, and as intending to go on to Nicopolis, "for there I have determined to winter." In his last reference to himself in II *Timothy* he seemingly has been rearrested, for apparently he is back in Rome, and again in bonds and awaiting execution. "The time of my departure is come."

All this makes so clear and reasonable a picture that one could wish it were indisputably true. But the difficulties are so serious, these conjectures cannot be accepted unquestioned. First, the order of events is obscure. Did Paul go to Spain before he revisited his Aegean churches or after? It cannot be ascertained. Moreover, we have no certainty as to the order in which the Pastoral letters were written. This smooth-running story of Paul's last days depends upon a I *Timothy*–*Titus*–II *Timothy* sequence. But any other arrangement is possible, thereby upsetting the whole neat tale. Next, the references to Paul's trip to Spain in *Clement* and the *Muratorian Fragment*, while explicit, are totally devoid of information. Beyond stating that he made the journey they say precisely nothing. Third, as we have seen, the Prison epistles more probably belong to Paul's earlier mission in Ephesus, rather than to his closing detention in Rome. Furthermore, the full authenticity of the Pastoral letters is too uncertain to permit working out Paul's last days in detail. Finally, Paul had said "goodbye" to his Aegean churches forever. His work among them he considered finished. He had set his face toward Spain. Only a major disaster could have called him back. Any return there is unlikely. Paul was facing west. But of this hope of evangelizing in Spain we have only Clement's vague whisper and the *Muratorian Fragment's* faint echo.

The conclusion is plain. With the close of *The Acts* all exact knowledge of Paul's closing experiences and movements ceases. All that comes down to us from the dim mists of the past is the universal tradition of his final, heroic martyrdom. This brave word is strongly verified by the great paean in II *Timothy* which has in it the ring of the true Pauline spirit.[1] "I suffer hardship unto bonds, as a malefactor." "Demas forsook me." "Only Luke is with me." "Take Mark, and bring him with thee." "At my first defence no one took my part, but all forsook me." This is our last glimpse of Paul, the aged—a lonely man, suffering in chains, deserted by friends, on trial for his life, sure of a fatal verdict, but waiting with triumphant courage, and bravely chanting his song of victory:

> For I am already being offered,
> And the time of my departure is come.

[1] Though it must be admitted that the meaning of "faith" as a deposit of belief, in the phrase "I have kept the faith," is not in accord with its meaning in the other Pauline epistles as the believer's response to the grace of God.

I have fought the good fight,
I have finished the course,
I have kept the faith:
Henceforth there is laid up for me
The crown of righteousness,
Which the Lord, the righteous judge,
Shall give to me at that day;
And not to me only,
But also to all them
That have loved his appearing.

So, "absent from the body, and . . . at home with the Lord,"
in pain and triumph, Paul entered into "glory," fulfilling
his deepest longing to "depart and be with Christ" who "is
all and in all."

Chapter 10

THE PRACTICAL SAINT

His Achievements—A Summary

"The slave of Jesus Christ."

WHEN PAUL on the Damascus Road saw a vision of Jesus, Christianity or "The Way," as it was known among believers, was a small Jewish sect whose adherents dwelt mainly in little Palestine. Its chief center was the Holy City, Jerusalem. Its leaders were the ten Apostles. Judas, according to *The Acts*, had died a mysterious, violent death soon after the crucifixion. James had been early martyred. The little church's accepted head was the staunch, cautious James, the brother of Jesus. Its leading spirit was the energetic Peter. As a movement it had spread north into Samaria, northeast into Syrian Damascus, and up the west coast through Joppa and Caesarea into northwestern Syria to Antioch. It was also reaching southward toward Egypt.

Its membership was comprised almost entirely of Jews. Included were many Dispersion Jews from distant parts of the Roman Empire, who had settled in Jerusalem. There were also some Samaritans, who were part gentile in blood, and strict adherents to the five books of the Law. A few gentile proselytes, like the Ethiopian Eunuch, had been baptized and received into the Fellowship. Fewer still were the outright gentiles, who, like the Roman centurion, Cornelius, under exceptional circumstances had been granted full admittance into the movement.

148

age-old convictions. Alone, Paul could never have won. Apparently Peter came strongly to his support. And the practical, all-powerful James gave his consent. Paul's victory was complete. Jewish Christians were to remain at liberty to continue their accustomed practices. But the gentile Christians as full members of The Way, were to be forever free of such requirements.

Though Paul triumphed, he soon found that a stiff minority repudiated the Jerusalem verdict. The "Judaizers" continued on his trail. Everywhere they stirred up fellow Jews, troubled the gentile converts, and bitterly persecuted Paul himself. But Paul never receded. Everywhere he declared the gentile freedom in Christ. Everywhere the Gospel continued to spread. At his mission's close, what he had found as a narrow Jewish sect, Paul left as a flourishing world religion.

Third, by his letters Paul sealed the work begun in his churches. As we have seen, it was his way of keeping in touch with them, untangling their problems, curbing their excesses, strengthening them in their weaknesses, teaching them further truth as it is in Christ Jesus, and uniting them in the bonds of fellowship. If he had done only this by his letters, they would rank as among the most effective epistles of all time. But great as were these achievements by his pen, they are the least part of all which Paul's writings accomplished.

Actually in them he gave the Christian movement its beginnings of an inspired literature. Not that Paul thought of himself as writing holy scriptures. That never entered his mind. At times he stated openly that what he was dictating was specifically not the word of God, but merely his own best opinion. His knowledge, he said, was partial. "For we know in part." But future believers came to recognize that here in his letters, often so rapidly and casually tossed off, was a new, inspired writing, a Christian literature.

Furthermore, his writings embody a carefully wrought-out systematic Christian theology that can be accurately plotted and set forth. Also, that theology has been basic to all true Christian thinking from Paul until now. Even more, it has been the means of repeatedly renewing the Gospel's transforming power to men and movements down the centuries. Paul thought out, more profoundly than any man, the basic principles of God's nature and actions as revealed in human history and the life of Jesus. He worked out so thoroughly their implications to Christian experience and practice that his insights and injunctions have never been bettered. He, beyond all others, except for insights in the Johannine writings, best interpreted the meaning of Christ for the heart, the mind and society. Inevitably his letters became a part of Christianity's inspired literature.

These are the magnificent achievements of Paul. The Christian movement by an adequate technique spreading its challenge across the Empire! A Jewish sect set free to become the world religion for all future ages! The implications of God's grace in the life of Jesus, and the transforming experience in Christ put upon a solid intellectual basis! What other Christian, since the wondrous movement began, has achieved half so greatly?

Of course others wrought while Paul worked. Other believers became missionaries. Some got to Rome and evangelized there effectively long before he arrived. Some, too, had thought searchingly on the Gospel's meaning. When Paul was converted, much profound thought had already been given to the meaning of God in Christ. Others, too, toiled, suffered and risked their lives for Christ's sake. Not all that Christians so marvelously achieved in the first thirty years after the Resurrection was wrought by Paul alone. But their heroic stories had no fortunate biographers. Paul we know. And while these early victories were not due entirely to him, they were largely so. As compared with other brave souls of his time, he was "in labors more abundant."

But *achieve?* Paul would never admit, except when his apostleship was being disparaged, that he ever achieved anything. Indeed, to achieve was exactly what he could not do. "For I know that in me . . . dwelleth no good thing." "Wretched man that I am!" All that he achieved was the grace of God working in him through Christ Jesus into newness of life. "For me to live is Christ." "I thank God through Jesus Christ our Lord."

How much Christ and his Gospel wrought and achieved in Paul is plain when one contemplates how farreaching were the effects of this newness of life in the chief apostle. Paul's central convictions may best be characterized by the one word *new*. The presence of Christ in him made all things new.

A new God! As a good Jew, Paul repeated the creed, "Hear, O Israel: Jehovah our God is one"—the only God. He was "the God of Abraham." He was "the God of Israel." He was the God "who led us forth out of the land of Egypt." But most of all, he was the stern God of the Law, the absolute, implacable, sovereign Judge of men and nations. The Psalmist had sung, "Like as a father pitieth his children, so Jehovah pitieth them that fear him." The prophet had declared, "As one whom his mother comforteth, so will I comfort you, saith the Lord." Paul had read and knew these, but they had never become central in his thinking about God. For Paul, God was the God of the Law, inexorable, righteous, judging.

But when Christ entered Paul's soul, God became new to Paul. The hard taskmaster of the Law vanished. The righteous heavenly Father stood revealed. "For ye received not the spirit of bondage again unto fear; but ye received the spirit of adoption, whereby we cry, Abba, Father." "Not . . . bondage . . . unto fear." All dread of the Eternal displeasure gone! Every worry about the intricacies of keeping the Law dispelled! Instead of an almighty legal enforcement officer, the divine Father. Henceforth Paul could begin his praying with the words given by Jesus, "Our Father."

A new Saviour was, of course, Paul's source of revelation that God is our Father. Instead of the long-expected messiah who should overthrow with crushing power the enemies of Israel, exalt the Chosen People, and compel the name of the one true God to be reverenced among all peoples, while he ruled in earthly glory, Paul now knew the blessed Redeemer. To describe his glory, Paul exhausted all the heavenly vocabulary he could command. By this New Saviour "were all things created, in the heavens and upon the earth." He was Lord, "far above all rule, and authority, and power," and over all created beings; the Glorious One before whom "every knee should bow." He was the one Saviour of men, who "brought life and immortality to light," and gave himself upon the cross for our redemption. He was the clear revelation of the true character of God, the one by whom we "have our access . . . unto the Father." And he was the goal of human history, for God will "sum up all things in Christ."

Of Jesus' earthly life it was his death and resurrection that gripped Paul's attention. Of his miracles Paul breathes hardly a word. Of his teachings Paul makes hardly a direct quotation. To incidents in the Carpenter's life he hardly refers. Anecdotes about the Nazarene he rarely relates. It is the cross and the empty tomb that hold Paul's gaze and enthrall his devotion. "He died." "He arose." "He emptied himself." "The power of his resurrection." Verily, for Paul, "God was in Christ reconciling the world unto himself." Here was a goodness and love that spared not itself, and a moral glory that could not suffer defeat.

This New Saviour meant also a New Presence. "For to me to live is Christ." "Christ liveth in me." "That Christ may dwell in your hearts through faith." God, Christ, the Holy Spirit, Paul never distinguishes in a clear doctrine of the trinity. He can speak as interchangeable equivalents of "the Lord the Spirit." But Paul, after the Damascus Road, knew himself to be "in Christ," and that Christ was, as he put it, "in me." Paul was at once the most practical and most exalted of mystics. He could write such down-to-earth injunctions as, "Be at peace among yourselves," "Let us not be weary in well-doing," and the exalted declaration, "Have I not seen Jesus, our Lord?" The glory of God was to him no longer a far-off wonder in the distant Eternal World, but the abiding presence of the indwelling Christ.

This New Presence of the abiding Christ transformed the believer into a member of the New Humanity. Instead of being a "natural man," he had become one of the "children of light." "If any man is in Christ, he is a new creature." He has a new mind, a new power, a new hope, and new instincts. He is delivered of his sins, fears, shackles and, as we would say, complexes. For Paul, the Christian is a new type of being. He is no longer merely a human being. In him now grew what was impossible in his natural state, the virtues of the Beatitudes, and the Fruits of the Spirit. He ceases to be of the earth, earthy. He belongs to the "colony of heaven." He is a human being lifted by the grace of God in Christ, here and now, to the divine glory. Not ambition but service, not pride but humility, not self but love. So has the believer been transformed by the spirit of the indwelling, risen Christ. In a twinkling, the glory of Christ had taken possession of him, and Saul became Paul, the son of the Law became the man in Christ, the persecutor of the saints became the evangelizing missionary. Henceforth Paul was the slave of Jesus Christ.

Being in Christ and a new creature or person, Paul found himself a part of the New Unity. Instead of Jew and Gentile, Paul now realized that God hath "made of one [ancestor or forefather] every nation of men to dwell on all the face of the earth." Racial, religious, social, even sexual distinctions lost all but formal significance for those in Christ. "There can be neither Jew nor Greek, there can be neither bond nor free, there can be no male and female; for ye all are one man in Christ Jesus." Broken humanity, split in a hundred fragments, Paul saw united, not by travel, enlightenment, economic necessity, or force of political pressure, but by Christ who unites the race by making men new creatures, children of God. They become new beings, a new race. The human race, Paul saw, will be united by being re-created by Christ into a New Humanity, new in nature, new in outlook, new in motive, above all earthly divisions. Humanity will be united in Christ, according to Paul, not by the obliteration of basic differences, but by being lifted up in character to the divine glory, where all divisive distinctions vanish. There will still be variety. There will still be "diversities of gifts." But there will be the blessed unity where all are "one body in Christ."

As one of the New Humanity, Paul gained a New Freedom. Instead of being under the Law, he was now under grace. It amounted to receiving a new religion. The galling shackles of religion by rule and righteousness by rote vanished. He had entered into a religion of grace, gratitude and intimate fellowship. Mechanics had been transfigured into life. The bondage of legal religion was broken. Henceforth men were called unto freedom. For freedom did Christ set him free. In that freedom he stood fast, bound never again to be entangled in any yoke of bondage. His was "the liberty of the glory of the children of God." "Where the Spirit of the Lord is, there is liberty."

The New Presence bringing this New Freedom brought also a New Dynamic, "the power of his resurrection," "the power of God unto salvation." Christ's abiding presence brought Paul the inexhaustible resources of heaven. No longer did he moan, "What I hate, that I do, . . . the good which I would I do not . . . to me who would do good, evil is present . . . who shall deliver me?" Rather he could shout, "I can do all things in him that strengtheneth me." He knew the joys of victorious living. He knew the surge of surplus moral energy. "We are more than conquerors through him that loved us." "If God is for us, who is against us?" "For I am persuaded, that neither death, nor life, nor angels, nor principalities, . . . nor any other creature, shall be able to separate us from the love of God, which is in Christ Jesus our Lord." "Thanks be to God, who giveth us the victory through our Lord Jesus Christ."

This New Freedom resulted in a glad New Conduct. For Paul, that conduct sprang from realizing that every man was "the brother for whose sake Christ died." "Love therefore is the fulfilment of the law." Therefore each is to "bear ye one another's burdens, and so fulfil the law of Christ." One is "not to think of himself more highly than he ought to think." But he is "so to think [of himself] as to think soberly." Always he is to be "in honor preferring one another." He is to give special consideration to the weak, the narrow-minded, the over-scrupulous. He is not to "put a stumblingblock in his brother's way, or an occasion of falling." "It is good not . . . to do anything whereby thy brother stumbleth." Always one is to "owe no man anything, save to love one another." The power that initiates the New Conduct, and keeps it vigorous, is the knowledge that "the brother" is one "for whose sake Christ died."

Such an experience brought forth a New Motive. Instead of merit earned by diligent keeping of the Law, the new motive was the compelling love of Christ. "The love of Christ constraineth us." Unceasing gratitude to Christ became Paul's unquenchable incentive. All his toil, suffering and devotion were but practical efforts to express his thanksgiving to God for the gift of his grace in Christ. The theme song of Paul's heart, the words of his preachings, the background of his letters, the diligence of his journeys, and the endurance of his sufferings was one glad, unquenchable thanks to God for his unspeakable gift.

Paul's greatest contribution was himself. That is always a man's chief achievement. Whatever else he may have accomplished—an invention, a book, a painting, a social reform—a man's best offering is always himself. Back of all he does lies what he is. The greatest thing about Paul was the soul of Paul. He is our supreme example of missionary toil, profound Christian thinking, highest ethical living, and practical sainthood. Many factors contributed to this.

He possessed a marvelous capacity for adjustment. In every variety of situation he contrived to get along. He could adapt himself to all sorts of men and circumstances: the manual laborers at Thessalonica, the party divisions at Corinth, the intensities of Ephesus, the friendships at Philippi, and the majesty of Roman officials everywhere. He could rejoice in abundance, be content in poverty, and remain at peace in illness. "For I have learned, in whatsoever state I am, therein to be content. I know how to be abased, and I know also how to abound: in everything and in all things have I learned the secret both to be filled and to be hungry, both to abound and to be in want." As his letters show, and as *The Acts* confirms, Paul could "become all things to all men."

He was a heroic and undiscouraged toiler. He carried out a world-encompassing mission in the face of persistent difficulties, dangers, opposition and persecutions. Yet nothing daunted him, turned him aside, or halted his endeavors. He endured dangers of geography: mountains, rivers, seas, seasons, and weather. He suffered the dangers of men: bold robbers, jealous compatriots, wrathful Judaizers, and brutal mobs. He surmounted dangers to health: cold, hunger, exhaustion, injuries, lashings, stoning, and imprisonments. He bore the burden of anxious toil: always supporting himself "with these hands," preaching, visiting from door to door, counseling and writing letters. He was, indeed, "in labors more abundant." Half sick, aging, weighed down with the "anxiety for all the churches," he accomplished all "in [Christ] that strengtheneth me."

He possessed a profound and elaborate knowledge of Jesus, gained by inquiry, study and experience. He had mastered the basic facts of Jesus' life, entered into experience with him as the risen Christ upon the Damascus Road, and thought through the meaning of the facts and his transforming experience.

Paul knew the basic facts of Jesus' earthly career. He could not help it. He had frequented Christian gatherings in Jerusalem where stories of Jesus were told in the beauty of their first freshness. As a burning convert, he needed a knowledge of Jesus' Galilean life as background from which to reinterpret his Messianic conceptions in the Old Testament, and to build his system of the Gospel. His epistles are proof of this. They reveal his elaborate knowledge concerning Jesus of Nazareth.

Of Jesus' earthly life, Paul knew that Jesus was "born of a woman." His was a completely human life. He knew that Jesus was "born under the law." He was a Jew, subject to the Law. He knew him to be according to the accepted belief, "of the seed of David." He was of the tribe of Judah and the ancient royal lineage. He knew he was "a minister of the circumcision." Jesus' mission was to the Jews. Paul knew of Jesus' "death of the cross." He was crucified as a malefactor. He knew that he "hath been raised on the third day." Paul knew the story of Jesus' resurrection appearances which he elaborates in great detail.

The fact that Paul could and did elaborate the resurrection appearances, and that in similar manner he related the story of the Last Supper in rich detail, compels us to admit that he doubtless could have told much else in Jesus' Palestinian career with equal thoroughness, had the occasion required. Indeed, in telling the Gospel story to gentile hearers, he must have done so. From the first, the Gospel included in part a telling of the relevant facts about Jesus.

Of Jesus' character, Paul knew of "the grace of our Lord Jesus Christ." He knew of his "becoming obedient even unto death." He also knew of the sincerity and purity that are in Christ. He knew, too, of "the meekness and gentleness of Christ." Paul knew of Jesus' unselfishness in that "Christ also pleased not himself." He knew of his utter and complete self-sacrifice in that he "emptied himself." To be sure, one finds here no miracles, no parables, and no sayings of Jesus. Yet here in summary is the whole career and character of Jesus. While Paul would have abhorred a Christ after the flesh only, he knew the story of that earthly life and its significance for his Master's risen glory.

Paul was a profound and persuasive preacher. Like all great preachers he had a fearless disregard of the consequences. The picture in *The Acts* is almost appalling. Persecuted out of Pisidian Antioch, stoned out of Lystra; beaten, jailed and banished from Philippi; mobbed out of Thessalonica, ridiculed out of Athens, mobbed again in Corinth, rioted against in Ephesus, and almost lynched in Jerusalem. Yet fearlessly Paul preached on! Disregarding details, the essential truth of this picture is confirmed by his letters. Usually Paul preached at the risk of his life.

He is also represented in *The Acts* as using every ingenuity to make his message effective. At times he was 'wholly absorbed in preaching.' Often he was 'discussing.' At other times he was found 'emphasizing' the Good News. Sometimes he appeared as a 'herald.' At other times he 'persuaded' or 'taught.' Thus by varied methods best suited to differing circumstances, he became "all things to all men, that I may by all means save some."

Always, Paul was a steadfast, sacrificing friend. He was deeply devoted to persons whom he knew, loved and remembered by name. What a procession of names troops through his letters! Timothy, Silas, and Titus, his "fellow-workers" in Christ. Stephanas, Fortunatus and Achaicus, whose coming rejoiced him. Salutations go to Aquila and Prisca. Euodia and Syntyche are exhorted "to be of the same mind in the Lord." Tychicus will make known "all my affairs." Onesimus is "a brother beloved." Aristarchus is "my fellow prisoner." Mark and Justus send greetings, also Epaphras. Luke and Demas "salute you." Encouragement is sent to Archippus. And *Romans* 16 is little more than a long list of names to whom Paul earnestly wished to be remembered. To these Paul sent greetings of devotion, advice, gratitude, encouragement, appreciation, endearments and "tears." Paul never forgot a friend. In the bitterness of his travels and the loneliness of his imprisonments he clung to them with deep emotion.

Finally, Paul was a mystic saint. He was radiant with God. For him to live was Christ. He was subject to mystical visions. They appeared almost inevitably when he was facing some stern crisis. *The Acts* and his letters together record some seven such exalted visitations. Some of these seven may overlap, so we cannot be sure of the exact number. Paul doubtless experienced many more. Upon the Damascus Road he saw a vision of the Risen Christ, where "as to the child untimely born, he appeared to me also." A little later in the Temple at Jerusalem: "When I had returned to Jerusalem, and while I prayed in the temple, I fell into a trance, and saw him saying unto me, Make haste, and get thee quickly out of Jerusalem." Still later in Corinth, after being driven from the synagogue, "The Lord said unto Paul in the night by a vision, Be not afraid, but speak and hold not thy peace: for I am with thee." Again, after his near lynching in Jerusalem, when it looked as though his dream of reaching Rome had vanished forever, "the night following [his appearance before the Sanhedrin] the Lord stood by him, and said: Be of good cheer . . . thou [must] bear witness also at Rome." On the voyage to Rome, when the terrible two weeks' storm threatened all with shipwreck and drowning, Paul brought courage and sense to the drenched crew and passengers, "Be of good cheer: for there shall be no loss of life among you. . . . For there stood by me this night an angel of the God whose I am, whom also I serve, saying, Fear not,

162

Paul; thou must stand before Caesar: and lo, God hath granted thee all them that sail with thee." At some time during his life, while wrestling with his "thorn in the flesh" he had received the assurance "My grace is sufficient for thee." In another exalted moment he had been "caught up even to the third heaven," where he had heard things "unspeakable . . . not lawful for a man to utter." He also experienced rapturous moments in Christian fellowship meetings where the joy of the Lord so burst upon him that he could affirm, "I thank God, I speak with tongues more than you all." Throughout his career Paul was in repeated mystic union with his Lord.

The perfect consummation of this mystic fellowship, which he pictured as the supreme joy of the Eternal World, plainly had already begun in him here and now. In the midst of physical pain incredible hardships, countless distractions and heavy cares, Paul had already begun to experience the glory of heaven. He was in Christ, so that "for me to live is Christ, and to die is gain." And there we leave him, where he so longed to be, and at last fully came "to be absent from the body, and to be at home with the Lord," in Christ who "is all, and in all."

A PAULINE DICTIONARY

EVERY READER of Paul should have before him a Pauline dictionary. The words Paul used did not always mean to him what they mean to us. Therefore, it is necessary to know Paul's definition of his own terms. Such definitions present difficulties. Sometimes Paul used the same word with several meanings, just as we do. We must learn to distinguish these differences. Also, Paul used words with meanings we do not have. So we need to learn new meanings for familiar words, and to remember them when we read his letters. Finally, Paul wrote in Greek, and most persons can read him only in translation. Unfortunately, our standard English translations do not always use the same word when translating one of Paul's terms. Any one of several words may be used for a single word used by Paul. This confusion can be considerably lessened by reading Paul in some modern translation, which usually interprets his terms in closer equivalents to our own.

The following definitions do not constitute a complete list of Pauline words. Nor do they give a full discussion of the words defined. But the list is complete enough, and the definitions full enough to give the reader a fair knowledge of Paul's most important meanings.

Age: or World. For Paul there are two ages, or worlds. (1) 'This present evil age,' the world and ongoing of history in which we now dwell, which is under the power and slavery of evil, and waiting to be delivered. (2) 'The age to come,' when with the swift, triumphant return of Christ, a new era will be inaugurated, in which evil shall be vanquished, creation delivered, the saints exalted, and Christ shall rule supreme.

Atonement: This is not a Pauline word in any sense. Nor is it properly a New Testament word. It occurs nowhere in the original Greek. It occurs only once in the King James Version, in Romans 5:11, where it is a mistranslation of a Greek word meaning "reconciliation." Christ did not make atonement to God, thereby appeasing him. Rather, through Christ we are reconciled, or won to God.

Baptism: This has nothing to do with the amount of water used, or the method practiced, though immersion was the common practice. (1) It was a ceremonial act by which the convert was initiated into the fellowship of believers. (2) A mystic, symbolic dying and rising with Christ, a mystic sharing in the sufferings and triumph of Jesus, thereby becoming at one with him. Going down into the water was 'dying' with Christ. Coming up out of the water was being 'risen' with him. Symbolically, the believer came to share the whole experience—baptism, crucifixion, burial and resurrection—of Christ. (3) Coming into a new, higher plane of living by taking on Christ's own life and character. See Romans 6:1–14.

Blood: "The blood of Christ." With Paul the blood has not of itself redemptive value. With Paul, we are not 'saved by the blood,' as though had no actual blood been spilt we could never gain salvation. What Paul means is that Jesus died a violent death. The death, not the actual blood, of Christ is involved in our salvation. It is the means by which we learn of God's saving grace, and become reconciled to him.

Body: Paul uses this word in four senses. (1) As do we, of the physical body of flesh and bone. "There is a natural body." This body is the dwelling place of "the inner man." Paul makes no sharp distinction between these. They are bound together. This body, through Adam, has become the tool of Sin, through which Sin and Death operate to destroy the person and the race. (2) As we never use the word, by body Paul means the whole personality, the self, what one means when one says 'I.' "Present your bodies a living sacrifice" is misleading. 'Present yourselves,' or 'Present your whole being,' or 'Consecrate yourselves to costly service.' (3) As a word to describe our heavenly existence. "There is a spiritual body." Since "the body" and the "inner man" were inseparable, Paul could not believe in a disembodied spirit. For the new existence in glory, God would give the inner man a new body, incorruptible, and "as pleaseth him." It is Paul's emphatic way of insisting upon the permanence of personality. (4) As the "body of Christ," or as we would say, the Church. See definition of the *Church*.

Church: With Paul, never a building and never a sect. Always a group of persons who have accepted Christ by faith. The Church is a corporate personality, all the believers being together one person in Christ. Paul thought of the Church under many figures:

a. *The Body of Christ*: A biological term: "So we, who are many, are one body in Christ." Paul calls the Church a body for several reasons: As the soul animates the flesh, so Paul thinks of the personality of Christ as animating the group of Christians which are his "body"; as the head is the directing center of the physique, so Christ is the head directing the body of believers. The Church as "the body of Christ" is the larger incarnation of Christ, through which he continues to operate in the world. Thus it is an organism, an organization or group of persons with a common experience in Christ. Like different parts of the human body, they share life together and perform varying functions for the welfare of the whole group.

b. *The Fellowship*: A business term, meaning a partnership. "Ye were called into the fellowship [partnership] of his Son." Here the Church is a society of gathered believers, like partners who possess common property or enterprise, and share the labors and the profits. So the Church is in partnership with Christ, sharing together with him and with each other the labors of the Kingdom and the rewards of salvation.

c. *The Building of God*: a construction term. "A building from God." With a foundation laid by Christ, and with Christ as "the cornerstone." With materials of "hay," "wood," "stubble," "silver," "gold." Here the Church as a group of believing people is a structure fitted together to be the dwelling place of God.

d. *The Home of God*: A family term. "Ye also are builded together for a habitation of God." This "household" is used by God as a home. It pictures believers as gathered together in the deep familiarity of a family circle with God as the Father, and head of the home.

e. *The Ecclesia*: or Gathered People of God. A social term. An ecclesia was any public assembly, a gathering of people from the public mass for a specific purpose. Hence the Church is the ecclesia, the gathering of people who have surrendered to Christ.

f. *A Cultivated Field:* an agricultural term. "Ye are God's husbandry," or cultivated field. A group of people upon whom God has worked, like a farmer upon his fields, plowing, planting, cultivating, harvesting. All involving time, labor, patience.

g. *A Letter of Christ:* a literary term. "Ye are an epistle of Christ." It is by the Church, the people of God, that the world reads Christ's message to men. It is by the Church that the members of Christ's body themselves learn to read and understand Christ's message. The Church unfolds the mind of Christ.

h. *The Heavenly Luminary:* an astronomical term. "Among whom ye are seen as lights in the world." The Church, like the sun, moon and stars, is to give light and direction to darkened mankind.

i. *A Work of Art:* a cultural term. "For we are his workmanship," or 'poems'—poems being a general word for a work of art, of skill, symmetry, beauty. The Church is usefulness, plus beauty!

j. *The Shrine of God:* a religious term. "Know ye not that ye are a sanctuary [the inner shrine] of God?" "We are a temple of the living God." Ancient temples had an inner shrine, a holy of holies, where God's presence was thought to be most real. So the Church is the inner shrine, the supreme place where God dwells and is made known to men.

k. *A Colony of Heaven:* a political term. "Our citizenship is in heaven," or better, 'We are a colony of heaven.' The Church is a colony living far from the mother country, but whose life, rule and practice is like that of the home land, heaven. It attempts to transform all about it into the likeness of the native land. It sets all its patterns of life by the heavenly home country.

The Church, with Paul, is the gathering of God's people in Christ, the nucleus of the New Humanity, the redeemed in Christ.

Communion (Fellowship): Originally a business term for a partnership, with common possession of property, labor and rewards. See *Church*, which is such a communion or fellowship.

"The communion of the Holy Spirit" is more than the blessing of the Spirit. It is the sharing of common partnership in the Spirit, whereby we become one person in Christ. Paul knew no individual Christians. As individuals they grow and serve only in partnership, in "communion" together.

Covenant: The basic meaning is that of making a will. One could properly speak of the Old Will, and the New Will. A will involves two parties, he who makes it, and the person or persons to whom it is made. It is a bond or obligation.

The old covenant, or will, was between God and the nation, Israel. It was the covenant, or will, of the Law. God, so to speak, willed Israel the Law, which Israel was bound to keep, in return for which Israel would receive stated benefits. It is almost a contract. Or the word 'religion' could be substituted. The old covenant was the religion of the Law.

The new covenant, or will, is between God and whosoever will accept Christ by faith. God need not be sought, as in a quest. He has openly disclosed himself. He is not to be gained by mere ritual obedience. He has already obligated himself. It is a covenant of grace, a religion of God's free offer of himself to men through the reconciliation in Christ.

Death: is not merely the cessation of physical life. It is that, and more. With Paul, Death is an entity, like Sin. It is a living power in league with Sin, that has invaded life through Adam's flesh, and is the ally of Sin bent on destroying the soul. "By sin came death." "The sting of death is sin."

"Dead to sin": is to be unresponsive to Sin. A dead thing does not respond when challenged.

"Dead in sin": is to be unresponsive to goodness.

Dying (and Rising): see Baptism.

Election: is Paul's word for opposing the pagan ideas of the Fates, and fatalism. So also are his words "foreknowledge" and "foreordained." "His people which he foreknew," "whom he foreordained." It seems to say that God has all things fixed beforehand, as fatalism and the Fates of paganism suggest. Nothing can be done. All is forever fixed. *But Paul means the exact opposite!* By these words Paul is asserting that God is free to act, he is free to deal with individuals. It is not a word suggesting any fixed divine plan, or the possible complete range of divine knowledge. It is a moral term stating that the Christian hope of salvation is absolutely certain. God has chosen from eternity, has always desired, or 'elected,' "foreknown," "foreordained" whomsoever will to be saved.

Faith: is man's way of obtaining God's free grace as manifested by Christ. (1) It is trusting God enough to let him act. It is our moral surrender to God's goodness. It is our receptivity to the divine grace. (2) It is also the result of our trusting to the free goodness of God. That is, accepting God's goodness by faith brings added faith that God is unshakably good. Thus faith brings more faith! (3) Faith is the believer's admission of his inability to attain the Christ-like life, and of his complete reliance upon God's sufficiency to create it in him.

Fellowship: see Communion, and The Church.

Flesh: is the physical body, and more. It is the physical body as the seat of man's perverted nature. It is man's lower nature as bent toward evil. As we say, "The world, *the flesh* and the devil." It is all the thoughts and impulses of our lower nature. To Paul, it is not that the physical body and its appetites are of themselves bad. But rather man's emotional and intellectual capacities are enslaved by Sin and made subject to "decay" and "corruption" of "this present evil age."

When Christ entered the world through becoming flesh, he battled Sin in the flesh. "Him who knew no sin he made to be sin on our behalf." By winning out over Sin in his whole lower nature Jesus, believed Paul, made it possible for us to gain victory over Sin and our lower nature, called "the flesh."

Foreordain: see Election.

Freedom: is the result of our surrender to God's free grace. It works out in several ways: (1) It unshackles us from the Law—from all conventional religious practices. (2) It frees us from the grip Sin and Death hold upon us through the flesh. (3) It liberates us from the power and fear of the cosmic evil forces: "angels," "demons," and "powers." (4) It brings a new sense of power, strength to conquer, unhampered by fear, petty rules, and personal weakness. The "liberty which we have in Christ Jesus" is the freedom which Christ discovered, lived, and revealed to us—freedom for holy living.

Gospel: This word has been capitalized throughout this book because in the New Testament it has a special, technical meaning. It stands for a specific set of ideas. In the Early Church it was not, as with us, a vague synonym for our religion as a whole. It stood for a definite sequence of ideas:

(a) The promise proclaimed by the prophets is now fulfilled.

(b) This fulfillment was heralded by John the Baptist announcing the immediate arrival of the Promised One.

(c) This proclamation of John's was fulfilled by the coming of Jesus of Nazareth as the Messiah, the Anointed One, and his preaching that the Kingdom of God was at hand.

(d) His mission was attested by many mighty works and much teaching.

(e) He suffered on the cross, he died and was buried, he rose again on the third day, he is exalted and reigns at God's right hand.

(f) He is coming again.

These points constitute the Gospel. They compose the Good News of the New Testament. Informed readers will recognize at once that all four gospels, the sermons in *The Acts*, and the message of Paul all follow this outline. In reading the New Testament it must be remembered that the Gospel is never a vague word, a kind of variant for 'salvation,' but rather this carefully articulated sequence of thought. Paul's own development of these points is set forth in Chapter VIII on "The Gospel Preacher." See also I *Corinthians* 15; 1–4, 11 for his condensed statement of these points.

Grace: Paul changed the Greek word for "greetings" into the Christian word "grace." He elevated a salutation into a benediction. (1) It is God's goodness acting toward men freely, unconditionally. It is a gift conferred by God upon men, the gift of reconciliation, of salvation. It is not earned, nor due, nor deserved. It is an outright gift. It is 'goodness you don't deserve.' (2) It makes God not a Law-master, but a Father, strong, loving, saving. It makes man not a subject, but a son, loving and grateful. It makes religion not mere routine duties and tasks, but a life of joyous gratitude.

Grace, then, is a kind of religion, as much as Judaism or Buddhism is a religion. It is a religion of God's free salvation accepted by faith, where life becomes divine living in joyous thanksgiving.

Glory: The quality of the Eternal World, the inner essence of God's nature. The light, so to speak, that dwells in God, in which God dwells, and which shines from him into our hearts, so that we, too, have glory.

Holy (Sanctified): to be consecrated, set apart, devoted to God. A Christian is wholly devoted to God, as a priest to the temple service. God makes us entirely his own, resulting in a character like his own. It is not a second act of Grace after conversion or justification, but simultaneous with it. When one accepts Christ by faith, he is made holy, set apart, consecrated to God.

In Christ: means the sharing of his presence, power, character and coming glory. It is to be so *en rapport* with Christ, that Christ's own life is reproduced in the believer. Since God is always present in his creation, men may have union with him. Faith in Christ, therefore, results in union with Christ. In this union with Christ we assimilate the nature and triumphs of Christ. We are "in him."

Joy: A high quality of Christian experience. It is neither pleasure nor happiness, which are at the mercy of circumstances. It is the steadfast assurance of God's fatherly goodness that makes life radiant under all conditions and experiences. It is the glad gratification of being "in Christ."

Justify and *Justification:* When one has by faith surrendered to the grace of God, he is justified. "Justify" is a law-court term meaning to acquit, to exonerate. "Justification by faith" means that God acquits us of the guilt of sin when we receive his grace.

This term conceives of God as a judge, upholding righteousness, but cancelling the penalty when the evil-doer turns to the court, and accepts the freely offered mercy.

Knowledge: not the knowledge of education, the learning from books, nor even from practical experience. Rather it is insight, understanding. The nature of religion is not the result of education or great learning, but of moral surrender. Knowledge, then, is insight into the spiritual appreciation of the Gospel, the Cross, and Grace. It comes by fellowship. It is given us when we come to be "in Christ."

171

In I *Corinthians* 8–10 it has the rather distinct meaning of 'enlightenment,' 'good sense,' or 'sensible.' Paul speaks of "growing in knowledge," that is, of increasing in insight and understanding of the full glory of the Gospel.

The Law: The whole Old Testament revelation given by God together with the practical interpretations by the great Rabbis. Like Grace, it is a kind of religion, a code religion of stern external compulsion to set standards and practices, imposed by God upon the nation, Israel.

Liberty: see Freedom.

Mind of Christ: To "have the mind of Christ" is for us to possess Christ's understanding of God, to know his attitude toward God, to understand God's concern for men. We thus know God and life as he knows God and life. It means Christ's insight into the principles of life and the nature of God, to have the Christ-possessed mind. Also, it means to possess that self-emptying humility that led Jesus to suffer "the death of the cross." It means, too, having "the mind of the Spirit [which] is life and peace."

Mystery: Originally a theatrical spectacle. Hence the Mystery religions which put on ritualistic spectacles of their gods, something on the order of modern Passion Plays. Through these "mysteries" deep truths were conveyed that the unitiated could not grasp. Hence, with Paul mystery becomes a term for God's saving grace as set forth by the Gospel. It was an "open mystery," for it was openly known and proclaimed. But it was also a "hidden mystery" in that to those outside its meaning was not clear, but was even "foolishness." It is not of this world, but is revealed by God. It is the hidden purpose of God, his ultimate purpose to save men in Christ. It can be grasped whenever one surrenders to God in Christ by faith. Then his eyes are opened.

The New Man: Having received Christ by faith, the believer becomes a member, as it were, of a New Race. Instead of Adam as a forefather, the founder of his race is now Christ Jesus. He has begun a new life in which Sin and Death have lost control. He is now transformed, and lives not after the flesh, but after the Spirit. His very constitution is changed. Instead of the lusts of the flesh, he now produces the fruits of the Spirit. He acts

172

from new purposes, with new motives, for new ends—the purposes, motives and ends of Jesus Christ.

Partnership (Sharing): covers both spiritual welfare and material goods. It is the basis of a far-reaching Christian communism, based on the principle of living not for personal gain, but for the enrichment of the community.

Peace: The believer sees Christ, sees the glorious goodness of God in Christ and, knowing that the heart of the universe is like God in Christ, ceases to fear. He fears nothing from God, for God is like Christ. He fears nothing from the universe, for the universe is the creative work of Christ. He fears nothing from life, for life is in Christ's keeping. He fears nothing from his fellow men, even malicious men, for Christ died for all men.

Peace is reconciliation to God and with one's fellow men. It is the assurance of being accepted by the Father as a son, that God is all Jesus showed him to be, and God will keep all committed unto him.

Propitiation: in Paul it does not mean a gift offered to appease an angry God. In Paul, propitiation equals forgiveness. Jesus is our propitiation in that he is God's gift showing us that the offer of forgiveness is freely presented to us by God's grace.

Reconciliation: bringing together into harmony sinful man and the gracious Father. That this reconciliation is possible and freely offered by the Father, was shown by Jesus. Hence we are reconciled through him.

Redemption: a legal term for freeing slaves. Literally it means to emancipate, or set free, and should be so translated. "In whom we have our redemption" means 'our emancipation,' our 'liberation,' our 'setting free.' The believer is liberated from bondage unto the Law; that is, set free from its external demands. He is emancipated from Sin, set free from its deadly power. He is freed as a slave is freed from his master, or an heir from a guardian, or a widow from her husband's authority. Freed from outside control to obey the new, divine, inner impulses.

Remission: a legal term meaning to cancel a debt, to remit a payment. So in "remission of sins," sin is as a debt which is cancelled, and is never to be collected.

Righteousness of God: This is God's free right to forgive, be clement, act mercifully, to save on his own terms, by grace instead of punishment. Not the righteousness of the Law, which was penal, but the righteousness of Grace, sending rain on the just and unjust alike, offering free forgiveness. It is God's eager effort to forgive and save men.

Saint: based on the root-word meaning holy, set apart, dedicated to God. Cognate words are holiness, sanctify, and sanctification. Hence, a saint is a holy or sanctified one, wholly consecrated to God through Christ. Hence, any earnest Christian; one who belongs to Christ. A synonym for being a Christian. Does not imply perfection, not faultless persons, but those who by the Spirit's power live in harmony with God in Christ and each other.

Salvation: a large term, never to be exactly defined. It means, in brief, all God has planned in Christ for man's total best welfare. It includes what the believer is saved from, which is servitude in every form; what he is saved to, which is sonship with the Father, and the New Life which reproduces in him the character of Christ; and what he is saved by, which is the life, death and resurrection of Jesus showing the grace of God offered in free, undeserved goodness.

Salvation: Paul speaks of it under many figures of speech. He pictures the believer as having been:

a. An *accused person,* now "justified," or acquitted. A legal, law-court term.

b. A *Debtor,* whose debt has received "remission," or been cancelled. A financial term of bankers and money lenders.

c. An *Enemy,* now "reconciled," reunited in peace. A social term of estranged, hostile persons now restored to friendship.

d. A *Slave,* "bought with a price" or "redeemed." An economic term for emancipation, liberation, given freedom.

e. A *Captive,* and "ransomed." A military term for one captured in battle and held as a hostage, but later ransomed, or set at liberty through payment by a friend.

f. An *Orphan,* who is "adopted," "made heir," given a share in the inheritance by the will. A family term, whereby an orphan or a slave is made one of the family with full rights of relationship, property and inheritance.

g. A *Devotee,* about to offer a sacrifice, seeking "propitiation" or "reconciliation." A religious term for restoration to the favor of the god. For the Christian, this is now forever unnecessary. Jesus by his death and resurrection has shown that God's grace freely accepts all who call upon him, and "sanctifies" or consecrates them to himself.

Note these are experience, not theological terms. Some of Paul's converts had been accused criminals, slaves, orphans and captives. Paul's figures of speech arose out of life experiences. They picture what had happened in the believers' souls by their new relation to God through Christ. These terms, then, are not theories of the atonement. Paul knows nothing about atonement in our popular sense. He speaks of reconciliation. Here rather are testimonies to God's saving grace in Christ.

Finally, for Paul salvation was cosmic in scope. It included not only man, but all created beings, and all nature, which now groans under the slavery of Sin and Death, and awaits the revealing of the sons of light.

Sanctification, and Sanctify: see Holy.

Sharing: see Partnership.

Sin: More than moral wrongdoing. A living entity that originally thrust itself into life, capturing control of humanity by seizing the "flesh," and through it the whole person of Adam, and through him passing down by inheritance through all generations of men. It is a great power of Cosmic Wrongness. It is also in league with its twin evil entity, Death. Together they work the complete ruin of all things.

Slave of Christ: which is the real meaning of "servant of Jesus Christ." A slave had few rights and few hopes. He could never please or serve himself, but only his master. Hence, to be utterly devoted, self-surrendered to Christ. Christ is the owner-master. The believer is Christ's for life, not pleasing and serving himself, but his Lord.

The Spirit: reproduces in the believer the character of Christ, which is outwardly manifested by the fruits of the Spirit: love, joy, peace, etc. Paul never depicts the Spirit as a third person of the Trinity. He speaks of the Spirit of God, Spirit of Christ, and "the Lord the Spirit."

The Spirit may also have any of three meanings: the Spirit of God, the human spirit, and the spirit as a disposition or attitude, as the spirit of enmity or holiness. Sometimes the three are more or less combined, as "standing firm in one spirit."

Tongues: Ecstatic utterances made by believers when under strong emotion in worship meetings. Often they sounded like the babble of some foreign language. It was looked upon as the speech of the heavenly world.

Wrath: Never the anger of God. Paul never speaks of God as angry. Always he is gracious. "Wrath" is Paul's word for God's unvarying opposition to human corruption, in lust, selfishness, and moral atrophy. Wrath is the automatic result of human sin. It is the disastrous effect of the universal moral order upon man for his evil-doing. Wrong-doing automatically incurs disaster. This disaster Paul calls "the wrath of God."

Paul never speaks of "the Judgment" or "the Judgment Day." He never directly mentions Hell. In their place he puts "Wrath" and "the day of wrath." For him the moral order is the will of God. The disasters which men suffer for their evil he sees as the result of God's direct action.

Much of what he calls wrath, we would now call natural and psychological law. But Paul's point holds: that when men do evil, at once they begin to suffer. This suffering is God's wrath, the perennial evidence of his unceasing opposition to evil, and his firm enforcement in the universe and human history of his moral order, where evil-doing always brings disaster.

But Paul may have a deeper meaning here. By Wrath he may mean nothing less than an attribute of God's inner nature. "The wrath of God is revealed from heaven" by the plight of humanity just as the love of God is made known by the Cross. The love of God, the righteousness of God, the holiness of God—these are among the divine attributes. Paul may be asserting that Wrath is likewise a quality of God's inner nature, made known to us by revelation. It is the divine quality that abhors and battles sin. It is the holiness of God in action against all evil.

World: see Age.

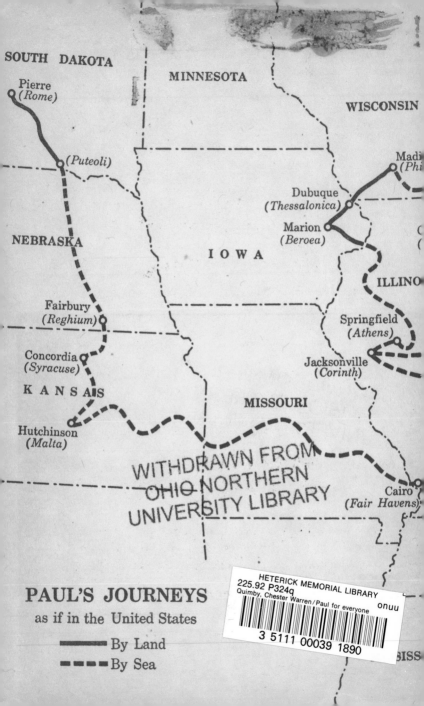

PAUL'S JOURNEYS

as if in the United States

━━━━ By Land

■ ■ ■ ■ By Sea